When advertising tried harder.

Copyright © 1984 by Friendly Press, Inc.
All rights reserved.

Published by
Friendly Press, Inc.
401 Park Avenue South
New York City, New York 10016
United States of America

Printed in Italy by Arnoldo Mondadori Editore Verona

Designed by J. Suplina/Black Book Studios

Library of Congress Cataloging in Publication Data

Dobrow, Larry.
When advertising tried harder.

Includes index.
1. Advertising—United States.
I Title.
HF57813.U6D55   1984   659.1'0973   83-82058
ISBN 0-914919-00-8

When advertising tried harder.

THE SIXTIES:
THE GOLDEN AGE OF AMERICAN ADVERTISING

BY LARRY DOBROW

FOR CAROL,
WHO ENCOURAGED,
AND ENDURED.

This volume is not intended to be a complete record of U.S. advertising in the 1960s, much less a history of the industry during that pivotal period. It's a newsreel, a kaleidoscope, an overview of ten years that changed the language and the look of advertising forever.

It's a series of impressions, recollections and conversations that identify, illustrate and, I hope, illuminate what in my opinion is the best work of many of the best people in the business at that time.

In the sixties I was a partner and creative director of a Washington, D.C., advertising agency, and an adjunct professor (part-time) of advertising in The American Univer-

sity's continuing education program. I can remember the impact that a man named Bill Bernbach had on both aspects of my professional life.

In my first and most important role as advertising agency head (most important because it paid the rent and afforded me the luxury of teaching), I was excited and dazzled by the "new" kind of advertising being done by Doyle Dane Bernbach, a small New York agency that appeared to be reinventing advertising. Oh, yes, like everybody else who cared about the creative side of the business, I could already pick a DDB ad out of any crowd. There was nothing like them for style, and wit, and intelligence. So at my own ad agency, I used these ads to inspire and stimulate everyone in my shop, including myself.

In my lesser role as teacher of copywriting and principles, and guide to students seeking to acquire an appreciation of graphics, I found all of my textbooks made obsolete by the work of DDB. This made my job of teaching both more difficult and easier.

Easier because we could bring a new Doyle Dane Bernbach ad into

class, place it alongside a comparable ad in the text and tell the students: "Look, this is the way you do an ad today—and in your text, that's the way it used to be done." The difference was that obvious and that dramatic.

More difficult because we were determined to teach this "new" advertising while we were in the process of mastering its concepts and techniques ourselves.

Today, twenty or more years later, I'm still excited and dazzled by Bill Bernbach's creative revolution. But in doing this book, I was also surprised at how difficult it was to locate much of the work I wanted to include. Even more, I was disappointed by what I learned about my own industry.

We have no sense of history. We have little or no feeling of obligation to preserve our best work for the benefit of new generations of copywriters and art directors. The overwhelming majority of agencies express no regret at not having archives, and have no plans to establish any. Worse, professional and trade associations—the very groups you'd think would care—have no programs to search out the work of the past, or collect the best of the present. In isolated situations, organizations such as the Art Directors Club of New York publish annuals and possess fragments of the past —some TV commercials of one year or another, for example—but no continuity or point of view regarding our heritage of advertising art and copy. And, no archival concept is evident.

Equally disturbing, of those few agencies and advertisers who for one reason or another preserved the history of their own advertising, many are reluctant to share their treasure—often for the most asinine, irrelevant or thoughtless reasons. And they recognize no obligation to the industry to do so. Such an attitude could be simply shrugged off as selfish, if we had galleries and theaters filled with graphic histories of advertising. We don't. Companies that still have their old, great work should be officially encouraged to make it available to all.

How, then, does one manage to publish a collection of work as remarkable as what you'll find in this volume? With great difficulty. By tracking down art directors and copywriters who so love what they do for a living that as a hobby they maintain private collections of their favorite ads. A copywriter like Dick Jackson and an art director like Dick Calderhead—coincidentally, former partners in an agency of the sixties —who independently made their extensive files available to us. And Norman Tanen, Jim Durfee, Ron Barrett and the CLIO Awards, all of whom volunteered their precious collections of many of the best commercials and ads of the sixties. We are grateful to each of you.

It's a simple fact that this book would have been impossible to attempt without the total cooperation of Doyle Dane Bernbach. How appropriate that the agency that started it all has a historical perspective of the role played by Bill Bernbach and the agency in shaping the creative revolution. Along with an impressive number of classic commercials and print ads that were readily available from the agency, there also came a spirit of cooperation and an understanding that DDB's archives are essential to any study of advertising in the sixties.

Then, there was Nancy Madlin, without whose patience, persistence and painstaking follow-through this book could not have been written. Whether smoothing out details with the troops at Doyle Dane Bernbach or ferreting out work from more obscure and reluctant sources, Nancy defined and refined the job of research assistant. She was just terrific.

There were important contributions made also by Stu Waldman, who simply refused to sit on the sidelines as a proper publisher should. A former advertising copywriter who practiced his craft in the sixties, Stu served as a knowledgeable and valuable sounding board. It was his sense of purpose and urgency that kept the project always moving ahead.

A final thought on the subject of preserving the best work of any era and of every era: a museum, gallery or official archive is needed for our industry. Without such an institution, one day someone else seeking to publish the work of a previous generation may find available resources inadequate. Only then will we realize the extent of this neglect.

Contents

THE
CREATIVE
REVOLUTION

1

Looking back, it wouldn't be too hard to imagine that for thirty years we'd been waiting for something to happen. From the non-stop enterprise and enthusiasm of the "roaring twenties" to the advent of the sixties, more than time had passed. So had a way of life.

The depression of the thirties hadn't allowed for much exploration or innovation. In the forties, progress was measured by advancing armies, not by our ingenuity. It might not have mattered anyway, since we were all products of a cautious, once-bitten depression mentality. Living well (in the suburbs, of course) and collecting things were the principal objects of desire. No surprise then that we spent the fifties restructuring our postwar world into a consumer society, concentrating mightily on material acquisitions.

So there we stood—after a decade of want, a decade of destruction and a decade of limited achievement—ready to greet the future. As a people, we were younger than at any time in our history, better educated, growing more mobile and extremely restless, and most important, we were optimistic.

As a result, it wasn't enough to merely enter the sixties. We exploded into this new era. We elected our youngest president, we adopted Britain's Beatles, we began the worship of youth and the exploration of space.

The pace was picking up. Everything was changing. Not gradually, and often not comfortably. Change in the sixties was different. It was more abrupt. For many, it was not easy to handle or understand. "Generation gap" entered the language. Depending on your viewpoint, change was either too demanding and impatient, or

Quality without compromise at a price you can afford: The Mercury Monterey 4-door Cruiser

Mercury remembers your pocketbook, too
(saves you money when you buy, drive and trade)

◄ THE ROOM YOU NEED, A PRICE YOU'LL LIKE. While many '59 cars have reduced trunk space, Mercury offers you a 6-foot-wideloading area that's easier to reach and use (up to 34.5 cubic feet in some models). While other cars have put the "squeeze" on legs, arms, and shoulders, Mercury offers comfort for 6 people, not just 4. The price? The Monterey shown above is in Mercury's lowest priced series ____ only pin money more than the top cars in the low-priced field.

STAYS NEW-LOOKING LONGER ____ PROTECTS TRADE-IN VALUE. Mercury's extra quality pays you back with extra savings. The Super-Enamel finish never needs waxing, stays showroom-bright just by washing. Mercury brakes adjust themselves mechanically; no need to pay for periodic adjustments. Aluminized mufflers last twice as long as usual, cut replacement expense.

ECONOMY-POWERED ____ YOU SAVE ON GAS. Mercury's V-8 engines are America's newest, with up to 345 hp. A special Economy V-8 in the Monterey delivers extra miles from regular gas.

MERCURY DIVISION *Ford Motor Company.*

'59 MERCURY
Planned for People

SEE AND DRIVE THE BEST-BUILT CAR IN AMERICA TODAY ____ AT YOUR MERCURY DEALER'S

1958 *All car ads, even good ones like this for Mercury, were pure fantasy—before the creative revolution. Flattering illustrations or heavily retouched photographs were used to distort the look, length and lines of the car being advertised. This glitzy, glamorous imagery was accompanied by glib and often meaningless copy claims.*

exciting and unconventional. Like it or not, it was inevitable.

Most advertisers and their advertising agencies, though conservative by the very nature of their size and special interests, also recognized the need to be responsive to consumer attitudes and preferences which were changing dramatically. In fact, change does not adequately describe what was occurring in America. It was virtually a complete shift in standards and a challenge to traditional values.

It was all happening so fast that even advertising "experts" did not fully grasp the extent to which the nation was being transformed. In January 1961, a prominent advertising consultant and regular featured columnist for the industry's leading journal wrote a piece on the "ideal" copywriter. In enumerating fifteen qualifications—many of them basic requirements for holding down any kind of job, not just the specialized task of writing copy for an advertising agency—he included in his professional opinion the observation that men in their fifties, sixties and even into their seventies would be the best candidates. There was just no substitute, he believed, for experience. However true that may be, it completely ignored the fact that as we entered the sixties, suddenly almost fifty percent of America's population was under twenty-five years of age. Equally interesting was this high-priced consultant's description of his "ideal" writer as "modest" and "ordinary." At the very moment those lines were being written, more than a score of not-so-modest and far from ordinary copywriters and art directors had already fired the opening guns in the creative revolution. Most of them were barely out of their teens. So much for experience. Hello, energy. Welcome, talent. Bravo, audacity.

© 1962 VOLKSWAGEN OF AMERICA, INC.

Think small.

Our little car isn't so much of a novelty any more.

A couple of dozen college kids don't try to squeeze inside it.

The guy at the gas station doesn't ask where the gas goes.

Nobody even stares at our shape.

In fact, some people who drive our little flivver don't even think 32 miles to the gallon is going any great guns.

Or using five pints of oil instead of five quarts.

Or never needing anti-freeze.

Or racking up 40,000 miles on a set of tires.

That's because once you get used to some of our economies, you don't even think about them any more.

Except when you squeeze into a small parking spot. Or renew your small insurance. Or pay a small repair bill. Or trade in your old VW for a new one.

Think it over.

1960 *Then, along came the now legendary VW campaign, considered by most experts to be the best in the history of advertising. Gone were the lush settings, the artfully elongated automobiles, the beautiful models. In their place stood the "Beetle," unadorned and unretouched, and almost always in black and white. Most important, ads like "Think small" were achieving record readership scores. Simplicity was proving to be a virtue and relevance a far more powerful persuader than empty flights of fancy.*

While the nation was undergoing a true cultural revolution, the advertising business was involved in a genuine communications revolution. By the mid-sixties more than ninety percent of American homes had one or more television sets. To appreciate the stunning speed with which television captured the country one need look only as far back as the early fifties, when a mere ten percent of homes boasted a TV set.

A new kind of consumer was ready and waiting for something to get excited about. A new and more potent mix of media was in position and able to project commercial messages into more homes and in more ways than ever before in our history. Only two more pieces had to be fitted into place in order for advertising to realize its full potential in the sixties. First, someone was needed to lead the way into the promised land of the new creativity —a fresh, provocative, reality-based

creativity—to replace the fantasy-filled advertising of preceding decades. The old rules and the old ways just wouldn't cut it in the sixties.

Second, where would the new copywriters and art directors come from? Advertising agencies were very much like fraternal organizations—you were accepted upon presentation of the appropriate credentials, which often included attendance at the right schools and

connections in high places. Yes, there was Grey Advertising, the "Seventh Avenue" agency, which employed Jews, Italians, Greeks and other religious and ethnic minorities. But for the most part, the advertising business operated under an unwritten code that was rigid and restrictive. It was an uptight industry that sorely needed new blood and fresh ideas. The conventional buttoned-down minds that were in

The "Stirrup Cup" an ancient Scottish rite when the clan toasts the preservation of its land.

Does the stillman's knock hold the secret of Chivas Regal?

When you cross the white stone threshold of the Chivas stillhouse, you're likely to hear a curious tapping sound.

But not until you meet the head stillman, Albert Cruickshank, will you discover the true source of this sound. For Mr. Cruickshank regularly checks the stills by tapping the head of each with a small wooden mallet.

The mere sound tells his ear if all is

well within. As with his father before him, Mr. Cruickshank does not trust the perfection of Chivas Regal to anything but his inherited skills.

Could the secret of Chivas Regal's delicate taste lie here? Or perhaps in Strathisla Spring waters? Whatever, your first taste quietly informs you that excellence is present—Chivas Regal, Scotland's Prince of Whiskies.

12-YEAR-OLD BLENDED SCOTCH WHISKY · 86 PROOF · GENERAL WINE & SPIRITS CO., N.Y.

By appointment to Her Majesty the Queen, Purveyors of Provisions and Scotch whisky, CHIVAS BROS. LTD. of Aberdeen, Scotland. Established since 1801.

12 Years Old

In the late fifties, Chivas Regal advertising was handled by Young & Rubicam, generally recognized as the most creative of the large agencies. But even mighty Y & R, with all of its resources, had not yet adapted to a changing America.

This ad, so typical of the liquor advertising of the times, was pretentious and vacuous. Irrelevant copy was combined with a mélange of visual images—what were they trying to tell us?

After Doyle Dane Bernbach had been awarded the Chivas Regal advertising account, scuttlebutt had it that Young & Rubicam just couldn't believe the phenomenal readership scores registered by the new and deceptively simple Chivas advertising created by DDB. They confirmed it for themselves. It wasn't too long before the creative team concept was introduced at Y & R.

control of the business couldn't communicate effectively with the new, young, increasingly skeptical consumer of the sixties. As a result, agencies began to entertain the prospect of employing writers and artists who didn't fit into any previously known mold. Talent was fast becoming the principal requirement for landing a job in the creative department of most agencies.

At the same time, the pied piper of the new creativity appeared. His name was William Bernbach. His agency was Doyle Dane Bernbach. And the emergence of that agency as a powerful creative force, and of Bernbach himself as an inspirational and articulate leader, was the final link in forging the creative revolution.

In fact, so unique were the creative contributions of Doyle Dane Bernbach that for a few years, early in the sixties, it was commonplace to hear executives of major establishment agencies remark that there might be room on Madison Avenue for one "creative" agency, but it wouldn't be wise to assume that any others would or should follow their example. A few years later, however, virtually all agencies were under pressure to join the creative revolution.

As new creative agencies appeared, as copywriters and art directors emerged from anonymity, and as established agencies began to place more importance on their creative output (many at the insistence of their clients), advertising in the sixties underwent as complete a transformation as any industry in America.

The look, the practices, the techniques of advertising that had been evolving for more than sixty years, were swept aside or radically altered by the power and excitement of the creative revolution.

What idiot changed the Chivas Regal bottle?

When the Chivas Regal people changed their bottle recently, they were ready for some protests.

Not a storm of outrage.

At first, it does seem outrageous.

Why change a classic bottle?

A magnificent dark green bottle. And an antique shield that seemed to come out of Sir Walter Scott.

"It's a wonder they kept the shape," muttered one Chivas Regal fan.

True, the shape is the same. Still squat. Still jaunty.

Most important, the Scotch inside is still the same Chivas Regal. Not a day younger than 12 years. "Goode olde whiskie is a

Old.

heavenly spirit."

Then why change the bottle to clear flint glass? Why lighten the antique shield?

Because we live in an age of confusions.

One minor confusion is "light" Scotch.

People think of "light" Scotch

New.

as light in color. Color has nothing to do with "lightness."

People think of "light" Scotch as "weakened" whisky. Not so. Almost all Scotch is the same 86 proof.

True lightness is actually the "smoothness" of Scotch.

A light Scotch will go down as easily as water. Or honey.

No "back bite." No gasp. No wince. No shudder.

Many people consider Chivas Regal the smoothest (or lightest) Scotch in the world.

Why?

Since 1786, Chivas Regal has been made with the "soft" Highland Scotch of Glenlivet. (This

is prize Scotch whisky.)

Extravagant sherry casks are still brought from Spain for ripening it. (Each costs over £35.)

Chivas Regal is still the same clear gold color it has always been.

This color is what warrants changing the bottle.

Many people have never tasted Chivas Regal, because its clear golden color never showed.

Handsome though it was, the old dark green bottle made Chivas Regal look dark.

Some people translated this as "heavy."

Many people never saw Chivas Regal in a restaurant or bar.

The old dark bottle and label almost hid it.

Same great Scotch inside.

No longer.

The new clear bottle offers an uninterrupted view of Chivas Regal.

And a warm welcome.

Think of it that way, and it's not so idiotic, is it?

It's kind of brilliant.

12-YEAR-OLD BLENDED SCOTCH WHISKY. 86 PROOF. GENERAL WINE AND SPIRITS CO., N.Y., N.Y.

Isn't it risky for a well-established, top-selling brand to change its package? Of course it is! Isn't there a possibility that customers will turn away from a product that appears to be unfamiliar? Of course there is!

Then why mess with success? America was starting to signal its switch to "light" beverages. To anticipate the market, Chivas decided to change from a dark to a clear bottle. While trying to win new converts, unless they were extremely careful and clever, the brand easily could have forfeited its important market position. The fact that Chivas so successfully managed change can in good part be attributed directly to this brilliant piece of copy.

One word of the headline, "idiot," required hours of discussion. However, it correctly and precisely expressed the opinion of traditional Chivas customers, while disarming and charming them at the same time. The result was that Chivas not only never missed a beat, but the brand began to step along at an even faster pace.

Illustration and strong graphics, which had long dominated the appearance of most advertising, were replaced almost totally by photography, which generated a completely different "feel."

With Bill Bernbach showing the way, art directors and copywriters teamed up for the first time. All the elements of an ad were integrated into a single, relevant advertising communication. The message that emerged was witty and direct, the form was clean and simple.

For the first time, also, job opportunities opened up for some of those able to demonstrate the right skills, not just for those attending the right schools.

More than a few agencies actually encouraged originality, emphasized creativity and began to attract attention and even some important clients.

Creative ability and creative judgment had become prized commodities. Agencies and clients invested heavily in the new creativity, not always with equal or uniform success. Many did not understand the "magic" was in the idea, not in the technique. Nevertheless, virtually all agencies began teaming up copywriters and art directors. The traditional structure of the business had been altered, perhaps permanently. New ground was broken by these newly formed and liberated creative teams almost as a matter of course. It was a period unlike any other in the history of advertising.

Among advertising professionals then and now, there is unanimous—often reverent—belief that the Doyle Dane Bernbach agency was the unchallenged leader of the creative revolution of the sixties. It influenced the creative side of the business as no other agency, before or since, ever has. Conversations with dozens and dozens of agency principals, art directors, copywriters and others active in the industry for at least the last twenty years—in the U.S. and abroad—reveal a remarkable unanimity of opinion about the overwhelming impact on the advertising world of this one relatively small agency, as it entered the sixties.

Although there was some indication of what was to come, as the decade dawned there was little in the size or stature of Doyle Dane Bernbach to even hint at the influence it would have on the look, the feel and the direction of advertising throughout the sixties and for countless years to follow.

There may be no better example of the radical changes brought about by the creative revolution than this exceptional ad for Canada Dry beverages. It introduced a totally new strategy and campaign for a soft drink company not previously distinguished for its advertising, prepared by an agency not previously distinguished for its creativity.

J.M. Mathes, the agency, was an extremely profitable, very solid member of the Madison Avenue "establishment." By the mid-sixties its creative department had been recast by an infusion of Italians and Jews. This ad, with its exceptionally effective layering of art, copy and photography, was a textbook execution of the "new advertising." And the creative team—art directors Ralph Ammirati and Bill Arzonetti, copywriters Gabe Massimi and Eli Silberman—might not even have been considered for employment just a few short years before.

If your Harvey Probber chair wobbles, straighten your floor.

Every piece of furniture that Harvey Probber makes at Fall River, Mass. is placed on a test platform to make sure it's on the level. If you get it, it is. Mr. Probber loses a lot of furniture this way.

Mr. Probber's furniture has an almost luminous satin finish. It is produced by a unique machine that has 5 fingers and is called the human hand.

This luminous finish takes a long time to achieve, but it lasts a long time. The lovely chair above could be made with 14 less dowels, 2 yards less webbing, thinner woods and so forth. You wouldn't know the difference, but Harvey Probber would. Of course, in a few years you would know too.

NEW YORK/CHICAGO/DALLAS/BOSTON/ST. LOUIS/MILWAUKEE/NASHVILLE/HARVEY PROBBER DESIGN BOOK: ONE DOLLAR, DEPT. N610, HARVEY PROBBER, INC., FALL RIVER, MASS.

C an't make time to read the whole ad? It doesn't matter. George Lois and Julian Koenig, two of the shock troops of the creative revolution, provide all the information you need with a simple photograph and a short headline. It's a striking example of the creative teamwork that projected Papert, Koenig, Lois into instant prominence.

shop at Ohrbach's *MENS SHOP*

34TH STREET OPPOSITE EMPIRE STATE BUILDING · OPEN MONDAYS AND THURSDAY NIGHTS TILL 9

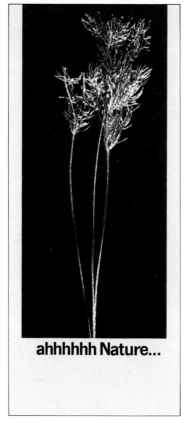

ahhhhhh Nature...

ahhhhh Choo!

Just because you have hayfever is no reason to sneeze. Take Allerest. This new tablet calms the cough, the tears, the runny nose, the itchy eye of allergy. It takes the sneeze out of hayfever. (Effective? You may be tempted to wear ragweed as a boutonniere!) Created for allergy and only for allergy. Allerest is the first drug of its kind available without a prescription. No cold tablet can work as well. Your druggist has Allerest and will tell you about it. 24 Allerest tablets for only $1.25

ALLEREST

A different breed of cat.

And what a difference it can make for you! Because it's different in engineering. Different in performance. Different in appearance.

You can be an adventurer at will in a Jaguar XK-E, for you command power which can produce better than 130 mph. You can be the subtle type, for your XK-E purrs through city traffic like a contented cat. And you are in good company, because Jaguar owners make up a roster of the world's most interesting people.

Only Jaguar can give you that relaxed confidence that comes with always being in complete command, whatever the road, speed or driving conditions.

More than thirty features are on an XK-E when you buy it. With many other sportscars they are added "extras." A few of these features are: the race-proven

engine; monocoque single-shell body; all-around independent suspension; four-wheel disc brakes; bucket seats fully covered with genuine leather; completely instrumented dash panel.

The Jaguar XK-E Coupe is $5,625 P.O.E., the Roadster $200 less. (If you're going to Europe, inquire about Jaguar's money-saving Overseas Delivery Plan.) There are Jaguar dealers coast-to-coast.
The Sportscar: Jaguar XK-E

S ynergism was the secret of the creative revolution. When art directors and copywriters worked independently, it is doubtful that concepts like these could have emerged. In these three examples, for Ohrbach's, Allerest and Jaguar, the words and pictures work together—beautifully.

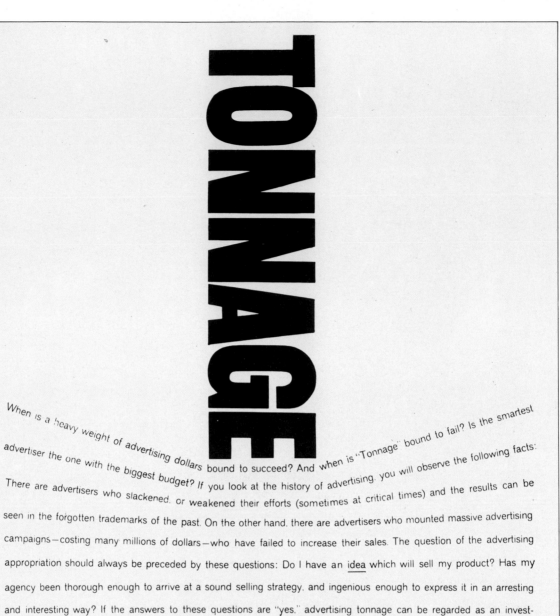

TONNAGE

When is a heavy weight of advertising dollars bound to succeed? And when is "Tonnage" bound to fail? Is the smartest advertiser the one with the biggest budget? If you look at the history of advertising, you will observe the following facts: There are advertisers who slackened, or weakened their efforts (sometimes at critical times) and the results can be seen in the forgotten trademarks of the past. On the other hand, there are advertisers who mounted massive advertising campaigns—costing many millions of dollars—who have failed to increase their sales. The question of the advertising appropriation should always be preceded by these questions: Do I have an idea which will sell my product? Has my agency been thorough enough to arrive at a sound selling strategy, and ingenious enough to express it in an arresting and interesting way? If the answers to these questions are "yes," advertising tonnage can be regarded as an investment, instead of an expense. Everything depends on the idea. Ideas sell products because—people buy ideas.

New York • Chicago • Detroit • San Francisco • Los Angeles • Hollywood • Montreal • Toronto • London • Mexico City • Frankfurt • San Juan • Caracas • Geneva   **YOUNG & RUBICAM • ADVERTISING**

Young & Rubicam, as befits an industry leader, used advertising on a regular basis to promote its services. This ad appeared in the early sixties and was one of the agency's most celebrated "house" ads. Although it won much praise at the time from the advertising community, it's interesting to note that the graphic device employed had its roots in the fifties, and the ad did not reflect the new look or apply the techniques of the creative revolution.

Isn't that Raquel Welch behind those Foster Grants?

(Yes indeed. See her in "Bandolero," from 20th Century Fox.)

To remove any further speculation, we'll own up. That is Miss Welch.

But, as you can see, our Foster Grants (known to many as the Sunglasses of the Stars) have done it again. They've given Raquel a new dimension. Several in fact.

One moment she's capricious. Then contented. Now candid. Even coy.

That, kind heart, is the Spell of the Shades.

Long, long ago folks wore sunglasses only when they were under the sun. Now they wear them from sun up till sun up. From New Year's Day till New Year's Eve.

In every kind of weather. Everywhere.

Sunglasses have become funglasses.

We can't tell you how happy that makes us, since Foster Grant is clearly the leader in the anti-glare business.

We have more styles in more colors than anybody.

And they all have ff77 lenses that meet U.S. Government standards for eye protection (standards a lot of expensive imports don't meet).

Now, if somebody mentioned sunglasses, who would you think of first?

Besides Raquel Welch.

"Am I doomed, C. B., to play the sex symbol in an age of flower children?"

© FOSTER GRANT LEOMINSTER, MASS

"So you admit you didn't come to Zermatt just to climb the Matterhorn."

"... and now, love, you know all my secrets."

"If you really wanted to hang on to Rhodesia, Sir Robert, why didn't you tell me?"

"Any man who straightens his tie as often as you just has to be hiding something."

"Matador, you're looking at a woman who wants more than a moment of truth."

The American public—no different from the rest of the world—adores its Hollywood stars. That's why celebrity endorsements almost always prove to be effective when they're believable. What could be more natural than a famous sex symbol hiding behind dark glasses in an attempt to retain some privacy? This campaign by Geer DuBois was so effective that for a while "Foster Grants" became synonymous with eyeglasses, and the entire headline—with the appropriate name inserted—entered the language for a few years.

Mitsouko by Guerlain

The Guerlain name appeared on many provocative scents—and ads—of the sixties, none of them more arresting than this page for Mitsouko. The daring close-up photography, dramatic cropping and innovative use of black on black won instant acclaim and created a timeless communication. Young talent with a bold new way of looking at the world—and advertising—was pushing the techniques and technology of the times to their very limits.

2

THE
GENERAL
AND HIS
TROOPS

2 How do you start a revolution? It may be simple, but it's not necessarily easy.

First, you introduce a philosophy that runs counter to established viewpoints and accepted practices. This generates a sense of excitement and poses an element of risk— all of which attracts young and adventuresome followers to the cause.

At the same time, you present a visionary's view of the way things should and could be. This wins even more new converts.

Finally, and with far more difficulty, you lead by setting a successful example.

In 1947, while still creative director of the Grey Advertising agency, a full two years before Doyle Dane Bernbach opened its doors and a good half-dozen before it began to earn some attention from the industry, Bill Bernbach fired the creative revolution's initial round with this well-targeted memo:

"There are a lot of great technicians in advertising. And unfortunately they talk the best game. They know all the rules. They can tell you that people in an ad will get you greater readership. They can tell you that a sentence should be this short or that long. They can tell you that body copy should be broken up for easier and more inviting reading. They can give you fact after fact after fact. They are the scientists of advertising. But there's one little rub. Advertising is fundamentally persuasion and persuasion happens to be not a science, but an art."

Bernbach was not opposed to the use of scientific methods, but he was against blind adherence to their findings. "All this is not to say," he continued, "that technique is unimportant. Superior technical skill will make a good man better. But the danger is a preoccupation with technical skill or the mistaking of

technical skill for creative ability." Bill Bernbach always believed that to light a creative spark, it was not enough to do the right thing. You could count on everybody else, all the technicians, to do the right thing. To make your advertising stand out, you had to do the inspired thing.

For one client after another, Doyle Dane Bernbach created advertising that stood out by following no formula, obeying no rules. Let others worship "the ritual," Bernbach believed in the god of inspiration. "We must develop our own philosophy and not have the advertising philosophy of others imposed on us. Let us blaze new trails. Let us prove to the world that good taste, good art, good writing can be good selling."

By 1960, Bill Bernbach had changed the lyrics, but not the tune. "A company will spend years in research and hundreds of thousands of dollars to create a point of difference for its product, and then use run-of-the-mill advertising to convey that difference to the people. Why? They must know that if their ad looks like all the others, their product will be classed with all others. So often the words are saying, 'Look how different I am,' while the total ad says, 'Pay no attention to what I say, I'm really one of the boys.'"

Certainly, throughout the fifties and well into the sixties, apparently

Bill Bernbach
1911–1982

better than anyone else in the business, Bernbach understood the synergistic signals that an ad could transmit to anyone within range. Readers and viewers who enjoyed the witty and intelligent communications directed at them by American Airlines, Avis, Chivas, Polaroid, Volkswagen, and other DDB clients came away with an impression of good and honest products being offered by good and honest companies. The advertising was so well made, it was easy to credit the advertiser with the same attributes. There's no doubt that many a perceptive company president or knowledgeable advertising director recognized the value of this intangi-

ble—but substantial—asset. Otherwise, how explain the prodigious growth of Doyle Dane Bernbach, during a period when most of the conventional wisdom on Madison Avenue was still debating the merits of the new creativity?

As advertising went charging into the sixties, Doyle Dane Bernbach had just completed its first decade. Writers and art directors at other agencies had for some time taken note of the agency's exceptional work for Ohrbach's and Levy's, Chemstrand and Polaroid, El Al and Utica Club. And DDB had just won the Volkswagen account. If you looked hard, the signs were there. But other than their penchant for winning gold medals in creative competitions—thereby achieving Bill Bernbach's clearly stated 1947 objective to "stand out in competition and not look like all others"—there was little to suggest that in the next ten years Doyle Dane Bernbach would join the select ranks of those agencies Bill Bernbach had described as "so-called giants of the agency field."

To properly comprehend what followed—that is, the extent of Doyle Dane Bernbach's extraordinary accomplishments during the

sixties—almost requires a suspension of disbelief. At the beginning of the decade, there were long-established advertising agencies that were ten times larger than Doyle Dane. These competitors—and they were tough competitors—were not tired or weak or inefficient agencies ready to pass from the scene. McCann-Erickson, J. Walter Thompson, Batten, Barten, Durstine and Osborn (BBDO) and Young & Rubicam—to name but a few formidable organizations—were growing, aggressive, powerful and intelligent companies themselves. They had impeccable credentials, excellent reputations, loyal clients, talented personnel and clout!

All the more remarkable, therefore, is that despite the entrenched position of the established agencies, Doyle Dane Bernbach grew almost at will. Despite the usual problems that accompany explosive expansion, there was no visible slackening of creative standards, no slippage or compromise in the quality of the agency's output. To the contrary, there is a conviction on the part of creative professionals that exists to this day, that during the sixties there was Doyle Dane Bernbach, and then there was everybody else.
When the decade of the sixties came to a close, DDB's

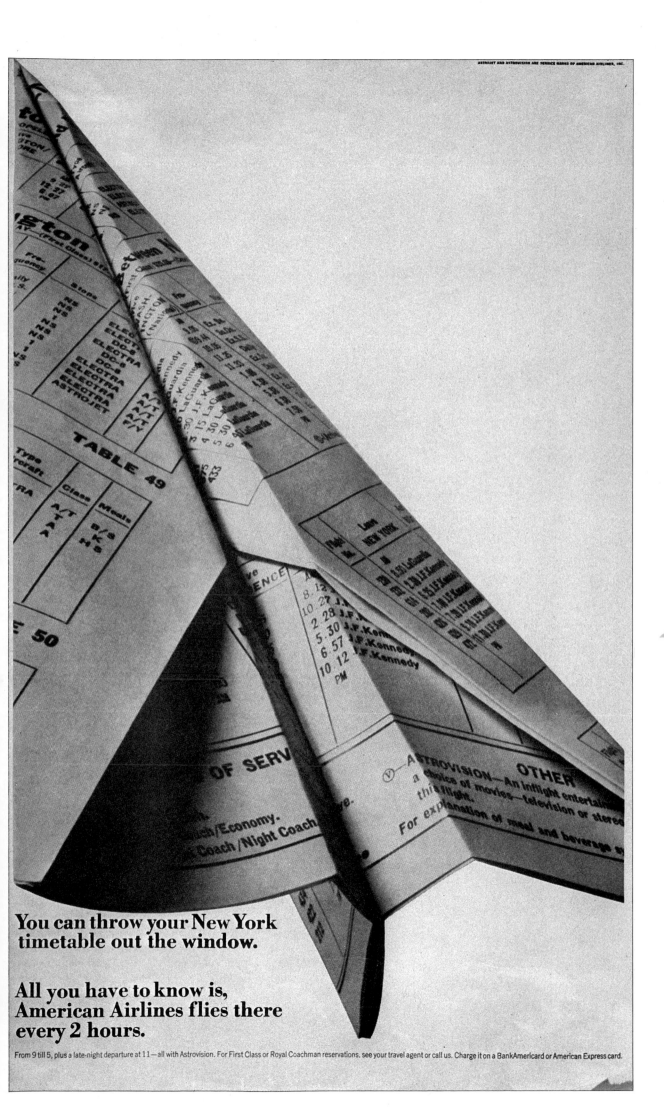

You can throw your New York timetable out the window.

All you have to know is, American Airlines flies there every 2 hours.

From 9 till 5, plus a late-night departure at 11—all with Astrovision. For First Class or Royal Coachman reservations. see your travel agent or call us. Charge it on a BankAmericard or American Express card.

billings had climbed from $25 million to an amazing $270 million annually. This, in a time when inflation and mergers were virtual strangers to the industry.

Yes, Bill Bernbach proved he could do more than create breakthrough advertising. He could also sell it. Most important, clients and the public loved it. Incredible as it seems, in ten giddy years Doyle Dane Bernbach had become the sixth largest agency in the United States and the seventh largest in the world. But as large as the agency had grown, it was as nothing compared to the size of its reputation and the extent of its influence. In many ways, Doyle Dane Bernbach was

the most powerful agency in all the world, and Bill Bernbach the most admired and respected individual in it.

Doyle Dane woke everybody up. The agency's string of stunning successes made a mighty persuasive argument for "the new creativity." As a result, more and more agencies came to the realization that the most important service they offered was not market research, media analysis, or other support functions—it was the making of an ad. In explaining the philosophy of his own agency to an industry group one day, Bill Bernbach said, "It is our belief that every other activity in our business is a prelude, however important, but just a prelude to the final performance, which is the ad."

On a similar occasion, Bernbach cautioned imitators: "Now that I have spent so much time urging freshness and originality, let me add quickly that doing it differently is not enough.

"This admonition is addressed specifically to writers and art directors. The recognition by management of the preeminence of creativity in advertising is not a license to be pretentious, or, to put it as unpretentiously as I can, it is not a license

to be phony—to do abstract acrobatics on a page. Your job is to simplify, to dramatize, to use all your talents to make crystal clear and memorable the message of the advertisement. The toughest part of our job is to tear away all the things that get in the way of that message. Yes, your ad ought to make a noise so that it will be noticed, but not a senseless noise."

The trick, according to Bernbach, wasn't in knowing *what* to say—every agency knows what to say—what makes all the difference is the *way* you say it. "Bringing dead facts to life and making them memorable."

By emphasizing creativity—by actively seeking, discovering and encouraging talent—Bernbach elevated the status and salaries of commercial artists and copywriters. Not just at DDB, but wherever they were employed.

Since power gravitates toward money, and the big money in the business was going to the men and women who could write or draw, Bernbach also permanently changed the pecking order within advertising agencies. When his own agency's unparalleled growth conclusively demonstrated that superior creativity was the most effective way to sell an agency's services, it followed that copywriters and art directors would soon become advertising's new elite.

When you're only No. 2, you try harder. Or else.

Avis can't afford to relax.

Little fish have to keep moving all of the time. The big ones never stop picking on them.

Avis knows all about the problems of little fish.

We're only No. 2 in rent a cars. We'd be swallowed up if we didn't try harder.

There's no rest for us.

We're always emptying ashtrays. Making sure gas tanks are full before we rent our cars. Seeing that the batteries are full of life. Checking our windshield wipers.

And the cars we rent out can't be anything less than spanking new Plymouths.

And since we're not the big fish, you won't feel like a sardine when you come to our counter.

We're not jammed with customers.

It didn't take long before most observers thought that they had the Doyle Dane Bernbach creative "formula" all figured out: big product photograph filling the top two-thirds of the page, with headline and copy occupying the bottom third. Imagine their dismay when, in 1962, DDB art director Helmut Krone designed a totally different look for what was to become one of the most successful advertising campaigns ever created. Krone's wonderfully fresh technique—first put to work with Paula Green's shrewd and saucy copy, and later with the clever, competitive phrases of David Herzbrun and others—helped attract readers. But it was the campaign's "big idea"—the No. 2, never-say-die underdog trying harder to _please_—that won customers.

As Bill Bernbach insisted throughout his career, most often when explaining the failure of others to copy his agency's "look," good technique was no substitute for a good idea.

Do you think the Volkswagen is homely?

The Volkswagen was designed from the inside out.

Every line is a result of function. The snub nose cuts down wind resistance. The body lines hug the interior workings. Nothing protrudes.

One Briton called the Volkswagen "a marvelous economy of design."

An American owner put it differently. "It's funny," he said, "how she grows on you. At first you think she's the homeliest thing you ever saw. But pretty soon you get to love her shape. And after awhile, no other car looks right."

The VW defies obsolescence. You can hardly tell the doughty shape of a 1950 model from a '61. To suggest altering it is heresy to owners. (Would you change the perfect form of an egg?)

But we are continually making changes you cannot see. Example: a new anti-sway bar eliminates sway on curves. Over a hundred such changes since 1950, but never in the basic design.

Is the Volkswagen homely? It depends on how you look at it (and how long).

Until the creative revolution, the objective of most good ads was to gain attention and interest. These Volkswagen ads, part of a landmark campaign, attempted to do more. They wanted readers to become involved. The ads were designed not to be complete without the

Got a lot to carry? Get a box.

Now add a few seats. Say 8.

Make an aisle so you can walk to the back.

Cut a hole in the roof to let the sun in.

Windows? At least 21. Doors? 5 should do.

Paint it up and what have you got?

The whole idea behind the Volkswagen Station Wagon.

active participation of readers. A reaction was required. Were they effective?
Once the campaign was launched VW sales never looked back. America
loved the ads—it learned to love the car.

The account executive, or account supervisor, the fabled "man in the grey flannel suit" of the forties and fifties, was no longer the key man and top earner of the sixties. More than anyone else, Bill Bernbach killed him off.

By merging the two disciplines of copywriting and art direction into one creative function—"the creative department"—the structure of most ad agencies was forever altered. The change was more than physical; it was also psychological. Artists and writers were brought out of the back room, the leash was removed, and direct contact with the client not only was permitted, it was encouraged. Lines of communication were

shortened. Less seemed to be lost in translation. The creative department was able to fight for its own ideas, to sell them and produce them. For creative departments, these were the golden years.

When it came to creative stars, as might be expected, Doyle Dane Bernbach once again showed its extraordinary strength. Other agencies might be happy to boast of even one of their artists making it all

Ned Doyle, Maxwell Dane & Bill Bernbach

Bob Gage

the way to the Art Directors' Hall of Fame. After all, in the entire history of the Club, only fifty art directors were selected for membership. Of those so honored, at the start of the sixties, four were employed at Doyle Dane Bernbach! The Hall of Famers were Robert Gage, Helmut Krone, William Taubin and George Lois. It is hard to imagine all of that talent in the same agency, on the same staff, at the same time. But the level of creative excellence at DDB was such that it was hard to choose between the talent of the legendary four and others who were constantly challenging them for recognition and choice assignments within the agency. Rick Levine, Bert Steinhauser, Jeff Metzner, Sid Meyers, Jim Raniere, Roy Grace, Len Sirowitz, Norman Tanen, the late Ira Mazer, and at least a half-dozen other DDB art directors were pushing the Hall of Famers and themselves to the outer limits of their creative abilities every day of the week.

But Bill Bernbach's ability to attract, spot and develop talent didn't stop at the art board. If anything, the agency's copy staff was even more celebrated than its art staff. In the sixties, the former Copywriters Club of New York had elected only nineteen copywriters to its Hall of Fame. Including Bill

Pee Wee Tee Vee

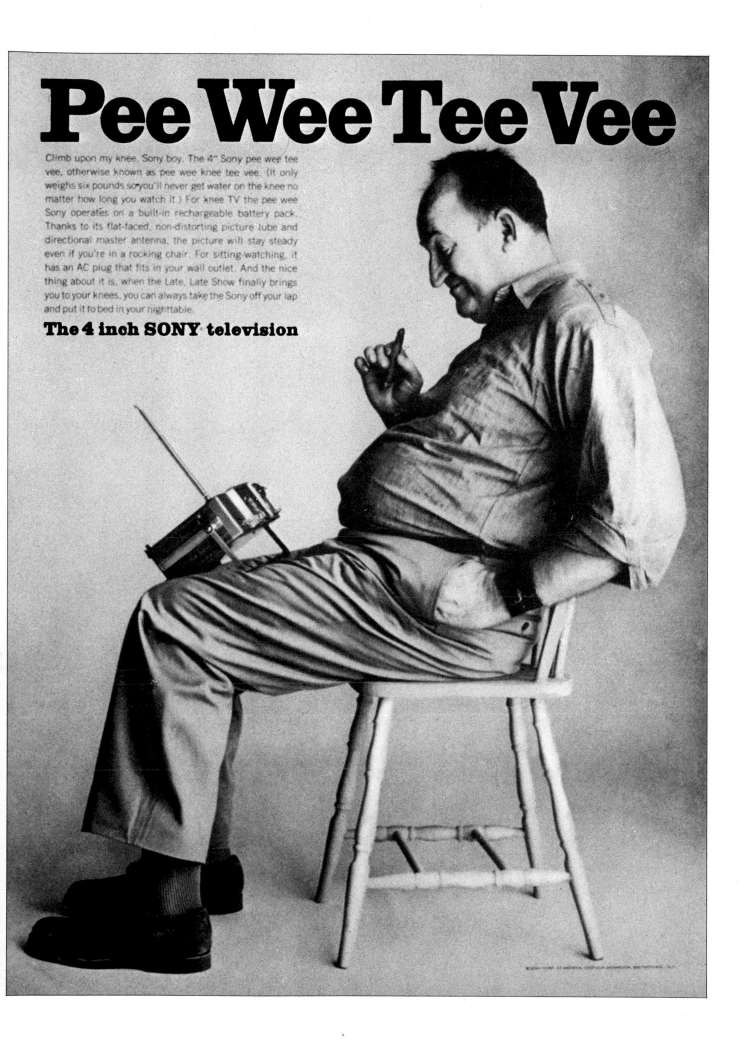

Climb upon my knee, Sony boy. The 4" Sony pee wee tee vee, otherwise known as pee wee knee tee vee. (It only weighs six pounds so you'll never get water on the knee no matter how long you watch it.) For knee TV the pee wee Sony operates on a built-in rechargeable battery pack. Thanks to its flat-faced, non-distorting picture tube and directional master antenna, the picture will stay steady even if you're in a rocking chair. For sitting-watching, it has an AC plug that fits in your wall outlet. And the nice thing about it is, when the Late, Late Show finally brings you to your knees, you can always take the Sony off your lap and put it to bed in your nighttable.

The 4 inch SONY television

Bernbach, six of the nineteen worked for Doyle Dane Bernbach! No wonder the agency's creative performance never slipped even during periods of frenzied growth. The talent was overwhelming.

The Hall of Fame copywriters were Phyllis Robinson, Julian Koenig, Mary Wells (Lawrence), Bob Levenson and Ron Rosenfeld. But that was only the tip of the copy iceberg at Doyle Dane Bernbach. Like a championship athletic team, they were two or three deep at every position. Other remarkably talented, award-winning copywriters on staff at the same time included Judy Protas, Leon Meadow, Paula Green, Dick Rich, Marvin Honig, Ed Valenti, David Herzbrun, Gene Case and enough others to start a dozen or so successful agencies—which they did, in time.

If you were a copywriter or designer selected to work at DDB in the sixties, it was much like being invited to join a team of superstars. You became part of an organization that possessed so much talent it almost never failed to make the right play at the right time, and as a result almost never lost any competition in which it was engaged—whether to win a new client or win another award. Within the agency, the battle for choice assignments never let up. The pressure was

Paula Green

Roy Grace and John Noble

Len Sirowitz and Bob Levenson

intense. The desire to prove yourself and excel in an environment so challenging and demanding resulted in each individual realizing his or her full potential and performing at the highest possible level of creativity.

It was the toughest place in town to land a job doing ads. Despite this, or because of this, it was also just about the only place in town where anybody who was any good wanted to work.

Bill Bernbach didn't just inspire the creative revolution. He *was* the creative revolution. He initiated the concept of the creative team. He ignored the rules, if indeed there were any—and relied instead on talent, intuition and taste. He attracted the best and the brightest people in the business, and created an environment in which they invariably did their best work. Ability was all that concerned him when employing a man or woman. He didn't see race, religion or sex. He made advertising relevant and witty and original.

No revolution in history has ever succeeded without a leader who was charismatic, articulate and daring. The creative revolution was no exception. It succeeded because Bill Bernbach had all the qualifications. He led the way, cutting so wide a swath, it was easy to fall in step behind him.

abcdefghijklmnopqrstuvwxyz

At your public library they've got these arranged in ways that can make you cry, giggle, love, hate, wonder, ponder and understand.

It's astonishing what those twenty-six little marks can do.

In Shakespeare's hands they became *Hamlet*.

Mark Twain wound them into *Huckleberry Finn*. James Joyce twisted them into *Ulysses*. Gibbon pounded them into *The Decline and Fall of the Roman Empire*. Milton shaped them into *Paradise Lost*. Einstein added some numbers and signs (to save time and space) and they formed *The General Theory of Relativity*.

Your name is in them.

And here we are using them now.

Why? Because it's National Library Week—an excellent time to remind you of letters, words, sentences and paragraphs. In short, *books—reading*.

You can live without reading, of course. But it's so *limiting*.

How else can you go to Ancient Rome? Or Gethsemane? Or Gettysburg?

Or meet such people as Aristotle, F. Scott Fitzgerald, St. Paul, Byron, Napoleon, Ghengis Khan, Tolstoi, Thurber, Whitman, Emily Dickinson and Margaret Mead?

To say nothing of Gulliver, Scarlett O'Hara, Jane Eyre, Gatsby, Oliver Twist, Heathcliffe, Captain Ahab, Raskolnikov and Tom Swift?

With books you can climb to the top of Everest, drop to the bottom of the Atlantic. You step upon the Galapagos, sail alone around the world, visit the Amazon, the Antarctic, Tibet, the Nile.

You can learn how to do anything from cooking a carrot to repairing a television set.

With books you can explore the past, guess at the future and make sense out of today.

Read. Your public library has thousands of books, all of which are yours for the asking.

And add books to your *own* library. With each book you add, your home grows bigger and more interesting.

National Library Week, April 16–22

It couldn't have been the juiciest of projects: do an ad to promote National Library Week. After all, dull, dry, pedantic subjects invariably resulted in dull, dry, pedantic ads that nobody ever read. It was not the kind of work that a bright and ambitious creative team would want to be associated with. Except at Doyle Dane Bernbach, where no assignment was without some redeeming virtue. Here, art director Charles Piccirillo and copywriter Monte Ghertler provide a classic demonstration of Doyle Dane thinking and Doyle Dane technique: get directly to the point and permit nothing to detract or distract.

Starting
Dec. 23
the
Atlantic
Ocean
will be
20%
smaller.

Watch for the inauguration of the first jet prop service across the Atlantic, introducing the Bristol Britannia, starting Dec. 23.

EL AL
ISRAEL AIRLINES

Although not strictly an ad of the sixties, this 1958 El Al classic by Doyle Dane Bernbach provided a clear indication of why advertising produced by a team—copywriter and art director—was the most exciting creative development in decades.

VOICE OVER: We've asked you to put on a short sock the length most men wear, and Burlington's new mid-length sock. The mid-length uses

lycra in a very special way so it covers your shins, yet can't slip. Can't get that bumpy look.

Can't make it fall down.

Nope! You can't make Burlington's new mid-length sock fall down.

Your shiny shins will never show. Burlington socks. Just one part of Burlington Industries.

If it's anything to do with fabric we do it at Burlington. And we do more of it than anyone in the world.

Dear clumsy bellboys,

brutal cab drivers, careless doormen,

ruthless porters, savage baggage masters,

and all butter-fingered luggage handlers

all over the world:

have we got a suitcase for you.

Commercials that demonstrate product benefits—a technique frequently employed to advertise headache remedies, detergents and disinfectants—are not among the most beloved by TV viewers. On the other hand, these two commercials for Burlington Mills and American Tourister may be not only the most entertaining and unforgettable product demonstrations of all time, they simply may be two of the best commercials ever made—of any kind. Here, DDB smoothly transfers its print technique to TV, capturing the elusive and envied "Doyle Dane look." The product is clearly the "star." No background diversion, no visual distractions, not a single extraneous element competes for your attention. With great humor and in perfect sync—music, performers and voice-over announcers—each commercial memorably demonstrates a single important point of product superiority.

(LAUGHTER)

VOICE OVER: Cracker Jacks in the big pass-around pack for when the gang gets together.

In a bit of inspired casting, Doyle Dane Bernbach selected Broadway actor Jack Gilford to play the kid who never grew up. Viewers identified with the character, and each new commercial drew strength from a previously established identity—just the way print campaigns did.

THE
TRUE
BELIEVERS

3

Bill Bernbach provided an opportunity and presented a challenge to creative professionals of the sixties. Here was living proof that a copywriter or an art director could start an advertising agency on his own and make it big!

And Doyle Dane Bernbach was making it big. Despite the agency's success, Madison Avenue remained somewhat wary of their approach, convinced that it should not be emulated. More than one talented, hard-working creative team, after enthusiastically presenting its latest effort to management, was sent back to the drawing board with the admonition, "Where do you think you are? Doyle Dane Bernbach?"

As Bill Pitts, copywriter and co-founder of the Lois Pitts & Gershon advertising agency, was later to observe: "In 1960, although DDB had been on the scene for a dozen years by then, and had become the ad agency for Polaroid, Volkswagen, Chemstrand, and other auspicious advertisers, this first creative agency was perceived by the establishment as a freak, if not *the* freak in the business. Conventional wisdom in 1960 allowed for only one 'creative' ad agency in America."

All during this period, however, a second "creative" agency had mirrored the success of Doyle Dane Bernbach. Within the industry, the profile of Ogilvy Benson & Mather (soon to become Ogilvy & Mather) was much lower. But outside the industry, as far as consumers were concerned, there were no advertising profiles any higher than those attained by Schweppes' distinguished "Commander Whitehead" and "The Man in the Hathaway Shirt"—complete with his romantic and mysterious eyepatch. Yes, the public knew, and liked, and responded to DDB's advertising for Volkswagen, Polaroid, Cracker Jacks, and other clients—but they also knew and liked and reacted to OBM's advertising for Schweppes, Hathaway, Rolls-Royce, and others.

Although Ogilvy's work was among the most original and creative in the sixties, he had little or no influence on the creative revolution. He was admired by art directors and writers, but they made little effort to model their work after his. That's because David Ogilvy's methods and techniques were one hundred eighty degrees different from those of Bill Bernbach.

Why, among art directors and copywriters, were the two men and the two agencies viewed so differently? Perhaps the best explanation of that might lie in the backgrounds of the two principals. Bernbach had not only always been a writer, but also was idolized for creating the copywriter/art director "team" concept. He was viewed as pioneering, irreverent, and a fighter for ideas.

Ogilvy, on the other hand, was a researcher turned writer. By itself, that was sufficient to throw up a wall of suspicion. Research and creativity were rarely comfortable with each other, and hardly ever on a first name basis.

David Ogilvy was perceived as rigid and restrictive, and as a result, OBM was viewed as an agency that played by the "rules." They did, but the rules they played by were David Ogilvy's. They were unlike any other rules in effect at establishment agencies, because they weren't really rules at all. They were guidelines to creativity.

To Ogilvy, the word was king and the visual took a back seat. Market research, not inspiration, was his guide. And humor had little place in advertising. To creative people, Ogilvy's rules were strait jackets. They hindered rather than helped creativity. This didn't prevent creative people from cheering the success of his advertising and his agency, but they didn't follow his methods.

But in reality, how far apart were the views of these two new giants of the advertising industry?

Bernbach's "relevance" was Ogilvy's "research," and the conclusion that both precepts reach is identical. The product must be the centerpiece, the "hero," of the advertisement. Nothing less was acceptable to either man.

"Originality" to Bill Bernbach meant an essentially fresh and forthright approach to the art of selling. In no substantive way was this any different from David Ogilvy's "reality." Both men were proponents of good taste, and they genuinely respected readers and viewers.

The newest part of Salisbury Cathedral is its spire. It is over 600 years old.

How to hear the music of an old cathedral town

AFTER TRAVELLING all day, most people long for five simple things. A friendly welcome. A hot bath. A good dinner. A comfortable night's lodging. And *peace*.

Britain's great cathedral towns have provided these creature comforts for centuries. They still do.

Imagine arriving in Salisbury on the evening our photograph was taken. The first thing you notice is the peace. It isn't a dumb silence but a gentle harmony of sounds. The whirr of a lawn mower. The slippered footsteps of devout men. The creak of praying oaks.

You find your inn and the music changes. There's a promise of refreshment in the jolly clunk of beer pumps. A promise of good fellowship in the sunburned country laughter. And a promise of good cheer in the kitchen chatter of dishes. The menu looks so tempting that you hurry down to dinner and postpone your bath. Ah well.

Salisbury is only one of thirty great cathedral towns that offer the same sort of welcome. Some travelers plan their tours so that they stay at a cathedral town every night. It makes delightful sense. Ask your travel-agent.

For free color booklet, "Old Towns of Britain," see your travel agent or write Box 134, British Travel Association.
In New York—680 Fifth Avenue; In Los Angeles—606 South Hill St.; In Chicago—39 South La Salle St.; In Canada—90 Adelaide Street West, Toronto.

HATHAWAY'S MONK'S CLOTH IS POSSIBLY THE OLDEST NEW FABRIC EXTANT. SOLIDS AND STRIPES, ABOUT $9.00. WHITE, ABOUT $8.00.

Hathaway revives <u>Monk's Cloth</u>: the ingenious loom work of a 17th century Flemish weaver

ON a recent trip to Europe, Leonard G. Saulter, Hathaway's president, unearthed a most unusual fabric—first woven some 280 years ago by an unknown Flemish weaver.

"This," said Mr. Saulter, "would make some damnably interesting shirts."

Now you can judge for yourself. Hathaway's weavers have duplicated the cloth. The result: Monk's Cloth—an all-cotton Oxford that *looks* like plaited basketwork and *feels* remarkably soft and nubbly to the touch.

Hathaway tailors this uncommon stuff in their unique Club style. Which means you get a trimly *tapered* midsection—for a tidy fit from chest to tails. A gently rolled, button-down collar. And a pair of sensibly long tails that won't ride up around your middle.

As for colors, you may choose from shades of Copper, Blue, Corn or White. And from a multitude of brave, but well-bred, stripes.

For a free *Dictionary of Shirts and Shirtings*, and names of stores, write C. F. Hathaway, Dept. A7, Waterville, Maine. Or in New York, call OXford 7-5566.

"Never wear a white shirt before sundown!" says Hathaway.

Santo Domingo, Santa Maria and San Antonio. Photograph by Elliott Erwitt.

Puerto Rico: civilized a hundred years before the pilgrims landed

THESE ANCIENT figures are Puerto Rican *santos*—carvings of the saints. They are only eighteen inches tall and they are made of wood.

Yet, as they stand gravely in the Caribbean sun, they seem to possess an inner serenity that is uncanny.

The earliest Puerto Rican santos were carved by Spanish missionaries. The art survives. Humble. Sometimes almost naive. But it is an immemorial link with that lovely old culture that flowered in Puerto Rico over a hundred years before the pilgrims landed at Plymouth Rock.

Today you can see many beautiful santos, new as well as old, in Puerto Rican galleries. Look especially for the figures of the Magi. They are usually on horseback and have a quiet charm that is all their own.

Isn't it pleasing to know that the graceful traditions of Old Spain still pervade this lovely island? You may read about hotels and factories going up by the dozen. And they are. But you can still find tranquility in shaded patios —and the hush of devotion in cellar-cool churches.

The friendly people of this sunny land intend that you always shall.

© 1959 Commonwealth of Puerto Rico, 666 Fifth Avenue, New York 19, N.Y.

She's got two more cases of Schweppes Bitter Lemon stashed away in the trunk.

Is it cricket to hoard new Schweppes Bitter Lemon?

(No—but it's smart. Last year Schweppes almost ran out of the stuff.)

COMMANDER WHITEHEAD

YOU are looking at a *practical* girl. Last year, during the Bitter Lemon drought, even Commander Whitehead could spare her only a six-pack.

This year, she isn't taking chances. As you can see above, she's hoarding cases of Schweppes Bitter Lemon.

Bitter Lemon is the newest triumph of the House of Schweppes. It was an immediate sensation in England. In America, connoisseurs are drinking it as if there were no tomorrow.

Schweppes Bitter Lemon is a great *mixer*. You'll get a remarkably good drink when you mix it with gin, vodka, bourbon, rum—you name it. Schweppes Bitter Lemon is also the first *adult* soft drink. It has a tart, lemony taste. So sophisticated that it's the only soft drink children *don't* like. All the more for you.

The extraordinary demand for Schweppes Bitter Lemon goes on and on. So rush to your store now!

Caution: To get the real thing— make sure the label on every bottle reads *"Schweppes Bitter Lemon."*

Here are four of the reasons most creative professionals, though respectful and appreciative of David Ogilvy's extraordinary accomplishments, do not place him in the forefront of the creative revolution. These ads, each for a different advertiser, are just about identical in appearance. They adhere almost slavishly to Ogilvy's rigid requirements for building readership. The fact that each of these campaigns was successful appears to be more of a tribute to Ogilvy's genius as a researcher than to his creative abilities.

David Ogilvy's oft-quoted reminder to copywriters and art directors working for his agency was "not to underestimate the consumer, because she's your wife."

What about Ogilvy's "rules"? There was no conceit or caprice attached to any of them. If David Ogilvy had been an athlete he would have been described as "hard-nosed." He liked what worked. Ideas, no matter how sparkling, were meant to be molded and adapted to fit tested and proven creative specifications. Each component of an advertisement—headline, sub-head, photograph, copy, caption—was rated for its contribution to readership and evaluated for effectiveness.

Could copy that was long hold the attention and interest of readers? Did it sell better than short copy? Whatever the length of the copy, should sentences and paragraphs be long or short? Did it matter? If so, how much? How important was the design of an advertisement? Were certain layouts virtually guaranteed to gain more attention than others? Was white type on a black background easier or harder to read than black type on a white background? Did it really make any difference?

The objective of all of this effort was to build a body of knowledge that could be used to improve the work of Ogilvy's creative teams. David Ogilvy was in search of a "for-mula" which theoretically would enable his agency to create cam-paigns that were always successful. All they had to do was follow the "rules." There would also be a bonus in all of this. Negative factors would be identified and known, and could be avoided when planning creative strategies.

Researcher David Ogilvy supplied creative direction—or more properly, "do's" and "don't's"—to copywriter David Ogilvy. However, in his own way and through application of his own experience and intuition, Bill Bernbach had earlier come to many of the same findings to which Ogilvy's research had led him.

One final important difference: Bill Bernbach favored the use of wit and humor in advertising. It was a relaxing, disarming and effective sales tool, he believed. DDB enjoyed undeniable success with humor. In their skilled and sensitive hands, it was a persuasive and potent sales weapon. Despite this, David Ogilvy ruled humor out. He became convinced, as a result of his research, that "people don't buy anything from clowns."

The extraordinary growth of both DDB and OBM did not go unnoticed. In the case of high profile DDB, advertising industry manage-ment preferred to view that agency as an aberration, an exception; or, as Bill Pitts put it, "a *freak*," an accident not likely to recur. DDB was to be watched (one could hardly afford to ignore them), even admired, but not emulated. Copywriters, art directors and others interested in the creative side of the business, on the other hand, saw the light and attempted to follow it.

Most of Bill Bernbach's disci-ples never had the opportunity to meet "the master," but they wor-shipped him nevertheless. Wher-ever they might be employed, in large agencies or small, these bright young people were attempting to force change. Understandably, the larger and more influential the agency, the more likely it was to resist new ideas. Client service teams were not about to willingly abdicate the seats of agency power traditionally occupied by marketers and managers, and turn them over to flaky creative types. But opposi-tion to change could not prevent it from occurring. The time had come, even for the large and reluctant establishment agencies, to acknowl-edge that creativity was the new force in the business.

The irresistible process of change was given a further assist by a brilliant, brash and bumptious art director named George Lois. After an internship at staid and repressive traditional agencies and an important stop at design-con-scious CBS, he arrived at Doyle Dane Bernbach. He stayed just a year—but what a year. He won three prestigious art directors' show medals, an overwhelming perfor-mance by any standards, and he was ready. Ready to confound the experts by proving that more than one "creative agency" could prosper on Madison Avenue. More than that, even in his own shop, George Lois planned to continue as a

BEFORE

AFTER

A Coty Cremestick turned Alice Pearce…into Joey Heatherton.

POPPY LOVE
Wear it.
But watch it!

PINK ME UP
That's what it's called
That's what it does.

WET APRICOT
Much nicer than
dry apricot.

SUN SHIMMER GLOSSER
For come-hither
highlights.

And you thought lipsticks weren't important, eh?
Another Cremestick trick: they're moisturizing,
but they're never greasy.
And zip! They're on in a stroke.
Ask Alice Pearce.

Some luscious Cremestick colors: And:

Papert, Koenig, Lois

The Nauga is ugly, **but his vinyl hide is beautiful.**

This is the Nauga, and he is the greatest. Once a year he sheds his hide for the good of mankind. His hide, happily, is Naugahyde® vinyl fabric. Naugahyde: the prettiest, toughest, most versatile fabric known to man.

It can look like anything. Rich silk. Rough tweed. Shiny plastic. Brocade. Burlap! Bamboo, for heaven's sake. Any fabric man has made, Naugahyde can duplicate. (And it lasts about ten times as long.)

One problem. Certain careless, or indiscriminate salespeople think vinyl is vinyl. Uh uh. Don't fall for it. Just-any-old-vinyl is not the same as Naugahyde. We know it, and a few months after you buy it you'll know it, too.

So look for the imaginary Nauga's picture. It hangs on every piece of furniture made with real Naugahyde. If you can't find the Nauga, find another store.

Remember: the Nauga is ugly, but his vinyl hide is beautiful.
Naugahyde is Uniroyal's registered trademark for its vinyl upholstery fabric.

Naugahyde® *vinyl fabric*

Papert, Koenig, Lois

working, hands-on art director. No administrator's role for George.

In concert with two talented and highly respected copywriters, Julian Koenig and Fred Papert, a new kind of agency of the sixties was formed—Papert, Koenig, Lois. They had courage, and talent. In 1960, those were ideal credentials. No surprise, then, that within a year or two Papert, Koenig, Lois had established themselves as an agency with a tremendous future. Their work was so inspired that it reverberated throughout the industry. In little more than five years their billings had reached in excess of $40 million, but even before that, they had engaged in another innovative action by becoming the first Madison Avenue agency to go "public." In retrospect, it's interesting to recall the criticism that was showered upon them for what was, after all, only a business decision. Some reports had it that they were selling out the integrity and indepen-

dence of the whole advertising business. Today, with shares of almost all major agencies in the hands of outside investors, it points up the dangers and double standard imposed upon those who dare to be original thinkers and pioneers.

Papert, Koenig, Lois did not survive the sixties. Why this agency failed to remain in business, considering how fast and far they'd come, is the subject of another story. There is no denying, however, that in the sixties PKL was the first agency to understand that a creative revolution was underway, and that there was an important place in it for them.

The PKL start-up signaled the beginning of a creative ferment that continued throughout the decade. Although most of the establishment agencies undoubtedly hoped the creative revolution would go away, not all of them chose to ignore what was happening. Among the most notable of the agencies to recognize both its premise and its promise was Young & Rubicam. For a giant agency, Y & R was unusual in that it had always displayed more than a routine interest in the quality and relevance of its creative product. So it was not a complete surprise when, at the very start of the sixties, Y & R granted great power, and the authority to exercise it, to a youthful and innovative art director who would soon be appointed president of this huge organization. His name was Stephen O. Frankfurt, and he accepted his promotion as a mandate to initiate change. He knew, or at the very least, he sensed what had to be done at Y & R to sustain its leadership in a period when creativity would prove to be the most marketable of all advertising services.

Under Frankfurt's direction, Young & Rubicam embraced the creative team concept. In 1962, early in his ascendancy, he wrote: "If an ad looks good, that isn't enough. An attractive ad without an idea is just a decoration. Sure, the execution of any ad should be brilliant. Why not? But execution alone is not advertising. We encourage our art directors to think in terms of copy, much as every good copywriter thinks visually. It's not important where the basic idea comes from—it can come from the writer, the artist, or the elevator operator. The important thing is that the advertisement, to do a job, must have a basically sound idea. Truly brilliant execution invariably grows from such an idea."

Just as Frankfurt encouraged Y & R's copywriters and art directors to help each other think, so the rest of the industry began to dismantle its traditional, separate art and copy departments and convert them into "creative departments."

But the change was not just structural. By the mid-sixties, Charles Goldschmidt, the relatively young chairman of Daniel & Charles, explored the lasting effects of the creative revolution: "Most agencies today have consciously or unconsciously developed an acute awareness of the need to reevaluate their communication techniques," he wrote. "That is why," Goldschmidt continued, "there are increasing agency efforts to communicate more interestingly with the consumer. The next year or two should see this effort expanded tremendously. While it may be called a creative revolution, it is more a reshaping of the basic communication strategy of American industry.

"This same revolution in ad making has had a profound effect on the internal operations and finances of the ad agency.

"If Vodka has no taste, how come I can tell which one is WOLFSCHMIDT?"

Papert, Koenig, Lois

This is the diver of Acapulco. Some men say he is crazy. But he is not. He just likes to dive. He stands on the edge of a hundred and sixty foot high cliff and throws himself into nine feet of water. He does this eleven times each day. But Acapulco is like that. A little mad. A little wild. Starting July 1st Eastern begins the first non stop jet service to Acapulco. You can fly there from Kennedy at 6:55 p.m. Wednesdays and Fridays. Or you can fly via Mexico City on Monday, Thursday and

Saturday. Make this the summer you see Acapulco. A whole, wonderful week of it. And pay us later with Eastern's new Charge A Trip plan. It only costs about $17 a month complete with air fare. Ask your Travel Agent. Or talk to us at 661-3500 or at 621-9450 in New Jersey. Once you see the diver of Acapulco, you will never forget him. You will never forget Acapulco.

EASTERN

43

DEVIL: Ha, ha, ha, ha, ha. Lay's Potato Chips.

Crunch, crunch.

Ummmmm. I'll have another.
DEVIL: I said just one. Ha, ha, ha, ha.

et you can't eat one.

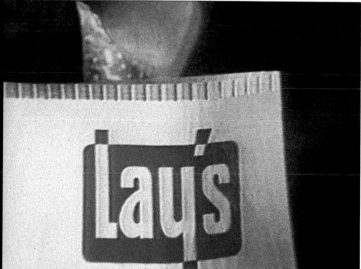

LAHR: Ha, ha, ha. Don't be absurd.

AHR: So you did. So you did. Ha, ha.
fiendish maneuver. Ha, ha, ha, ha.

VOICE OVER: Lay's Potato Chips. So thin,
so light, so crisp. You can eat a million of them.
But nobody can eat just one.

LAHR: De-LAY-cious.

A cowardly lion eating potato chips? Strange, strange thought. But Young & Rubicam employed the celebrated comedian Bert Lahr to convince the child in all of us. He had played "The Cowardly Lion" in The Wizard of Oz with such effectiveness that forever after he was identified with the role. He challenged viewers with the theme line, "Bet you can't eat just one." Nobody could, and the campaign roared on for years.

"In the matter of who does what, and for whom, in today's set-up, in an agency such as mine, for example, there is no longer an art department, no longer a copy department. There is a creative department with art directors who write copy and copywriters who do layouts.

"This creative breed is all too often temperamental and volatile. The care and feeding of this group is a full-time job. They're skittish, sensitive, naive, ambitious and dedicated in a weird way. They believe in advertising as a constructive force in our society. If it is not honest, it is a transparent piece of hokum. If it is meaningless, banal, or dull, don't ask them to be a part of it. They'll quit first. They want to believe in what they're doing, not because they're idealists, but because they have an intransigent faith in honesty."

There's no question that the general level of creativity was elevated. DDB was generating its own competitive pressures among creative teams within the agency, as well as increasingly capable competitors. The tougher the competition became, the more the work of DDB stood out from the rest. This can best be understood, perhaps, by the fact that their creative department wasn't just a collection of superb copywriters and art directors. It was an environment—a nourishing, encouraging, supportive environment, to which top management was totally committed. It was an agency in which the creative department called the shots. Experimentation and innovation were commonplace; so was the persistent questioning of traditional methods and techniques. Whether or not they understood what they were getting, clients came for the creative. They stayed because it worked. So when DDB account managers were handed a new campaign they were expected to sell it. Campaign concepts and execution were not subject to rejection.

Copywriters and art directors employed elsewhere may well have had equivalent talent, but often it was treated differently or even indifferently. In fact, many creative people, after leaving DDB, never reached the same level of excellence when working elsewhere. For them, the chemistry just wasn't the same, and neither were the results.

After all, working for DDB was the goal. It was what everybody wanted to do—the place where everybody wanted to be. The competition for jobs was incredible. Fortunately, growth never slowed for Doyle Dane Bernbach during the sixties. But despite the agency's frantic pace and ballooning size, they still couldn't find room for all who sought a place—even the most qualified. As a result, a lot of outstanding talent eventually got located at other agencies. These employees measured the quality of creativity and the support of management at their own shops against the standards and the legend of Doyle Dane Bernbach.

If you couldn't land a job at DDB, and if you couldn't realize your ambitions somewhere else, there was another option. You could try it on your own. At any other time starting a new agency was not always a viable choice. In the euphoric, creative atmosphere of the sixties, however, opportunities and prospects existed for those with entrepreneurial spirit. Most advertisers assumed other services would be provided; the one they really cared about was creative. In fact, it was not unusual for the client of an established agency, thrown into contact with his creative team, to encourage them to set up for themselves, in the hope he'd be able to command more of their time.

Given such encouragement, many copywriters and artists did something creative that they'd never figured on—they started a business. Research would probably have revealed that this particular group was the most unlikely to succeed. Few had ever had business training, were not interested in numbers and figures, and were comparatively undisciplined—characteristics not normally associated with successful business executives.

What's truly impressive, however, is that the always chancy decision to start a new enterprise proved to be the right move for a great number of them. Many creative boutiques of the sixties have grown into huge, full-service advertising agencies doing hundreds of millions of dollars worth of business each year, and in the process, have

What's the ugliest part of your body?

You just said, "my feet", didn't you?
That's typical.

Most women feel their feet are the least attractive part of their body.

Up until now all a woman could do was hide them.

But now there's something you can do to make them pretty.

Not just passable. Pretty.

Now there's a product named, appropriately enough, Pretty Feet.

Pretty Feet is a pleasant roll-off lotion.

Pour a little on your fingers every day of the week and rub it into your feet.

Then see the rough, dead skin roll right off.

Soon you'll have beautiful feet that can wear open sandals...lovely feet that won't hide in the sand at the beach...smooth feet that won't run stockings...soft feet that will be as sexy as the rest of you.

If you're genuinely interested in making the ugliest part of your body pretty, we'll be happy to start you off with a free sample bottle of Pretty Feet.

Just write to Pretty Feet, Dept. G2, Chemway Corp., Fairfield Road, Wayne, New Jersey.

Delehanty, Kurnit & Geller

themselves become members in good standing of the establishment. Out of all this only one thing is certain: none of them would employ someone like themselves to run their businesses.

No single decade before or since saw the number of important agency start-ups that took place during the "golden age" of the creative revolution. There had never been such a time before. There will probably never be one like it again. So much creative energy was compressed into so short a span of time that agencies which began life early in the sixties gave jobs and reputations to others who opened their own agencies, and were already well-established before the decade came to an end.

There couldn't have been a more appropriate way to signal the start of the sixties than the formation of Papert, Koenig, Lois. As previously noted, this new agency symbolized what was most exciting and different about the ad business. What a way for the sixties to take off!

In almost no time, 1961, another exciting new breed agency bowed in: Delehanty, Kurnit & Geller, guided by Shep Kurnit. They prospered, too, turning out terrific work like the classic Talon zipper campaign, and

taking on top young talent like Peter Hirsch, Jerry Della Femina, Ron Travisano and Neil Calet.

Another interesting agency emerged in 1961. When the year began, its name was Leber & Katz, and it was already celebrating its fifth or sixth birthday. Run by a successful businessman and accomplished copywriter, Leber & Katz quickly established itself as a solid and responsible addition to the New York agency scene. What it lacked was *flair*—which it acquired in 1961 in the person of Onofrio Paccione. The prolific, multi-talented Paccione—art director, designer, photographer par excellence— moved out of colorless Grey Adver-

tising and into the suddenly colorful and creative Leber Katz Paccione. Although the relationship proved to be short-lived—in just a few years the agency reverted to Leber, Katz & Partners, thereby salvaging all the initialled towels in the executive washroom—Lester Leber and Onofrio Paccione made some marvelous advertising together.

1962 saw two start-ups that proved to be durable and important. "The terrible Turk," Carl Ally, a creative fighter cast in the mold if not the likeness of Bill Bernbach, said goodbye to his favorite sparring partner, George Lois, and set up shop with Amil Gargano and Jim Durfee. McCaffery & McCall also

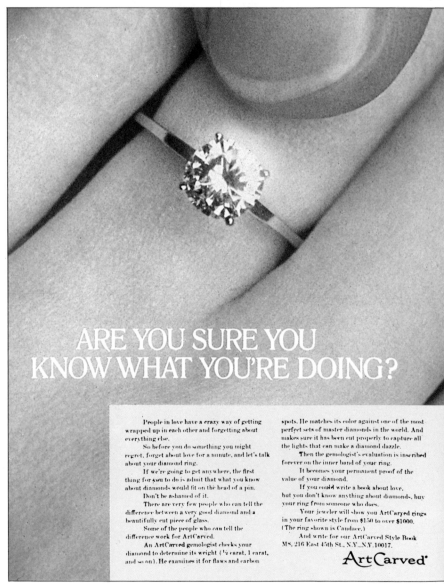

Delehanty, Kurnit & Geller

Of course it's good. Just look at that funky bottle.

took the plunge in '62. Both of these agencies, throughout their lifetimes, have been short on compromise and long on creativity—a legacy of their early sixties origins. In due course, Amil Gargano's name joined Carl Ally's on the company letterhead. Respect for tough creative selling, in the best tradition of the sixties, has characterized both of these blue-chip shops, and has proved to be an attraction for clients.

1963 marked the birth of Trout & Ries. Although this agency has never achieved the heavyweight status of so many others which opened their doors at approximately the same time, Jack Trout and Al Ries nevertheless gained considerable fame and distinction in the business. They are credited with being the principal developers of the strategy of "positioning," a creative concept that strongly influences marketing practices today.

In 1964, while many other big agency chief executives were busy belittling the "so-called young, hot creative agencies," Marion Harper of McCann-Erickson decided not to buck, battle or bemoan the trend. He joined it. He turned over separate offices, a set of keys, a checkbook and creative responsibility for the Alka-Seltzer account—and presto, Jack Tinker & Partners were in business. The pioneering, prize-winning advertising produced by Mary

Wells, Dick Rich, Stew Greene, and the rest of a very talented creative staff pulled together by Tinker would probably have never made it past the approval committees at the more bureaucratic McCann parent.

In 1965 it was the turn of Alvin Chereskin and Steven Rose to establish AC&R, an agency wedded to creativity. 1966 saw a memorable start-up. That was the year that Mary Wells, who earlier had been one of Doyle Dane Bernbach's prized young copywriters, departed Jack Tinker & Partners, where she had continued to build her considerable reputation. Leaving with her were copywriter Dick Rich and art director Stew Greene. Together they formed one of the most celebrated agencies of any era, Wells, Rich, Greene.

Mary Wells was talented, tough and very good-looking. Most important, her shop "clicked" from the start. The agency's brilliant work for Benson & Hedges 100's cigarettes provided the agency with an aura of success, and Mary Wells with an image that was a combination of Wonder Woman and glamour girl. It all seemed to be confirmed when she married client Harding Lawrence, chief executive officer of Braniff Airlines, who had moved his important account from Jack Tinker & Partners to Wells, Rich, Greene. Mary Wells Lawrence was perhaps the most successful product of the entire creative revolution. Among other things, many believe that for a considerable period of time she has been the highest paid female executive in the world. She is certainly among the most respected, and best known.

1967 was a vintage year. Three groups, all of whom were to become major creative agencies, first opened their doors in that year. Ron Travisano and Jerry Della Femina—a copywriter whose earlier

claim to fame came at a creative meeting for Panasonic when he suggested the line, "From those wonderful folks who brought you Pearl Harbor"—teamed up to form Della Femina Travisano & Partners. Give or take a few months, in the same year, Scali, McCabe, Sloves—with a few other principals—started their hugely successful agency. And also in '67, so did Lord, Geller, Federico, Einstein. Each of these three shops was founded by creative superstars of the sixties. Supposedly, they were anti-establishment free spirits who just could not be contained or restrained by traditional or conventional agencies. In turn, each has become a respectable and respected member of that same establishment today—while still creating advertising of exceptionally high standards.

After that exhausting burst of activity, new agency starts slowed down in New York in 1968. But on the West Coast a small new shop hung out its shingle for the first time. Chiat/Day was its name, and it, too, rode creativity all the way to the top.

1969 saw one of the few new start-ups by a woman when Paula Green, a much-honored Doyle Dane Bernbach copywriter, left the nest to establish her own agency. In 1971, in the afterglow of the golden age, another important creative shop revved up. It was the beginning for Rosenfeld, Sirowitz & Lawson, also products of Doyle Dane Bernbach, and like the others, they have enjoyed substantial success.

If by some impossible means Bill Bernbach had managed to persuade all those who loved him but left him, to stay, Doyle Dane Bernbach undoubtedly would have become the largest advertising agency in the world. But the industry was the healthier for the outpouring. The magic, the taste, and the knowledge was spread more rapidly as Bernbach's disciples moved around in the industry and struck out on their own.

If they run out of Löwenbräu.....order champagne.

Leber Katz Paccione, Inc.

Löwenbräu costs more than beer.

IMPORTED IN BOTTLES AND BARRELS FROM MUNICH, WHERE LÖWENBRÄU HAS BEEN BREWED SINCE 1383, BY HANS HOLTERBOSCH, INC. OF NEW YORK.
THE HAND-BLOWN LÖWENBRÄU CRYSTAL GOBLET PICTURED HERE IS AVAILABLE IN SETS OF 2 IMPORTED FROM GERMANY. FOR EACH SET MAIL $2.00
IN MONEY ORDER OR CHECK MADE PAYABLE TO CLASSIC IMPORTS, P.O. BOX 57, WESTBURY, N.Y. 11590. PLEASE ALLOW 4 TO 6 WEEKS FOR DELIVERY.

Leber Katz Paccione, Inc.

How to wind up a doll for Christmas!

Christmas is the time when boys get toys...and girls get mink. All the dolls open up their eyes and say "Evans" every time you mention mink. Our vast emporium of furs is a Santa Claus work-shop at Christmas. The busy Evans elves are making stoles and capes and jackets and coats to fill Chicago's stocking. Fur is the veriest, merriest present. And an Evans fur is the most. (Coat shown: Saga Dawn Pastel mink, $1,695 plus tax.) So isn't it clear? The key to Christmas is right in the door of 36 South State Street, where we live. **Evans**

PACCIONE

Leber Katz Paccione, Inc.

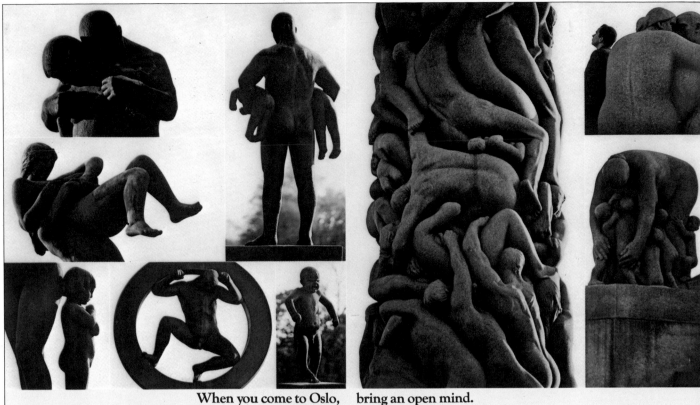

When you come to Oslo, bring an open mind.

Artists have been known to do strange things. But nowhere in the annals of art has an artist been known to do what the moody, energetic Gustav Vigeland did on May 1, 1921.

On that date, sculptor Gustav Vigeland sat down and signed away his rights to all future work his genius would produce.

He made the agreement with the city of Oslo. In turn, the city made it possible for Vigeland to devote all his energies to his art. They gave him a studio, provided him with materials, assistants and workmen.

Vigeland worked furiously. His ambition was to depict the full cycle of human life and all the love, hate, pathos, joy and agony that accompany it.

Over the years, the city ran out of funds a number of times but private fund-raising drives brought in millions to keep the project alive.

Did Vigeland attain his goal? Statistically, yes. Represented here are a few of the 1600 sculptures he finished before his death in 1943. They now cover over 108 acres of Frogner Park, their permanent home.

Artistic success? That controversy still rages. Some see nothing but a grotesque mass of writhing muscle. Others see a work so significant in scope that they compare it to Michelangelo's Sistine Chapel.

Make up your own mind when you come to Oslo. And you will form an opinion. Nobody who views Vigeland's work walks away from it unaffected.

And, we should add, nobody who visits Scandinavia leaves unaffected. It's a land of contrasts and controversy. A land of progress, yet a land where time stands still. There are contradictions everywhere you go.

Bergen, Norway, a small city of fishermen and merchants has supported a world-renowned symphony orchestra for over two centuries now.

The people of Copenhagen, one of the truly sophisticated cities of the world, hold up Hans Christian Andersen as their national hero.

Sweden has found a way to give her people total employment, near 100% literacy, cradle to grave security. Yet Sweden remains a democracy. The original Great Society, some say.

Let us have the privilege of introducing you to Scandinavia. We fly to Copenhagen, Bergen, Oslo, Stockholm, and Helsinki. We fly from New York, Chicago, Los Angeles, Montreal, and Anchorage. Within Scandinavia, within Europe, we serve more cities than any other transatlantic or transpolar airline.

Your travel agent will help you get more out of your trip. And if you'd like more information right now, just drop us a line: SAS, Dept. SXI, 138-02 Queens Blvd., Jamaica, N.Y. 11435.

SAS
SCANDINAVIAN AIRLINES SYSTEM

Carl Ally, Inc.

Old Bushmills Irish Whiskey can do anything, any time, any place.

If you want to know what goes into these holiday drinks besides Old Bushmills (yes, even the pink frothy one is a holiday drink—yes, it is made with whiskey), write to us. We'll send you the recipes.

If we missed your favorite holiday drink, make it with Old Bushmills anyway, then send us your recipe. We plan to do this again next year and we don't want to miss a favorite just because we don't know about it. And we

don't want you to miss Old Bushmills just because you don't know about it. Old Bushmills has burnished Scotch flavor without burnished Scotch smokiness—blended whiskey smoothness without blended whiskey blandness.

And if you're wondering why that whiskey straight, Whiskey Sour, Manhattan, Old Fashioned, whiskey on the rocks, and Irish Coffee are in the picture—well, as we said, Old Bushmills can do anything, any time, any place.

QUALITY IMPORTERS INC., 55 FIFTH AVE., NEW YORK 3, N.Y.

Carl Ally, Amil Gargano and Jim Durfee—all products of the creative revolution—demonstrated advertising's new look in this beautifully conceived and executed ad for Old Bushmills. It's hard sell in a soft package.

Tomorrow morning when you get up, take a nice deep breath. It'll make you feel rotten.

It is said that taking a deep breath of fresh air is one of life's most satisfying experiences.

It can also be said that taking a deep breath of New York air is one of life's most revolting, if not absolutely sickening, experiences.

Because the air around New York is the foulest of any American city.

Even on a clear day, a condition which is fast becoming extinct in our "fair city," the air is still contaminated with poisons.

On an average day, you breathe in carbon monoxide, which as you know is quite lethal; sulfur dioxide which is capable of eroding stone; acrolein, a chemical that was used in tear gas in World War I; benzopyrene, which has produced cancer on the skin of mice; and outrageous quantities of just plain soot and dirt, which make your lungs black, instead of

the healthy pink they're supposed to be.

At the very least, the unsavory elements in New York air can make you feel downright lousy. Polluted air makes your eyes smart, your chest hurt, your nose run, your head ache and your throat sore. It can make you wheeze, sneeze, cough and gasp. And because air pollution is responsible for many of those depressing "gray days," it may affect your mental well being. If you're a person who is easily depressed, prolonged exposure to polluted air certainly isn't doing you any good.

Of course, at its worst, air pollution can kill you. So far, the diseases believed to be caused, or worsened by polluted air are lung cancer, pulmonary emphysema, acute bronchitis, asthma and heart disease.

600 people are known to have died in

New York during two intense periods of air pollution in 1953 and 1963. How many others have died as a result of air pollution over the years is anybody's guess.

Who is responsible for New York's air pollution problem? Practically everybody. It belches from apartment buildings, industrial plants, cars, busses, garbage dumps, anywhere things are burned.

But the purpose of this advertisement is not to put the finger on who's causing the problem. It's to get you outraged enough to help put a stop to it.

What can you, yourself, do about air pollution? Not much. But a million people up in arms can create quite a stink.

We want the names and addresses of a million New Yorkers who have had their fill of

polluted air.

The names will be used as ammunition against those people who claim New Yorkers aren't concerned about air pollution.

If we can get a million names, no one can say New Yorkers won't pay the price for cleaner burning fuels, better enforcement of air pollution laws, and more efficient methods of waste disposal.

The cost of these things is low. A few dollars a year.

The cost of dirty air is higher. It can make you pay the ultimate price.

Box One Million
Citizens for Clean Air, Inc.
Grand Central Station, N.Y. 10017

IF YOU'D LIKE TO GET IN THE THICK OF THE FIGHT AGAINST AIR POLLUTION, SEND US A LETTER ALONG WITH YOUR CHECK FOR $2.00 (OR MORE) AND BECOME A MEMBER OF CITIZENS FOR CLEAN AIR, INC.

Carl Ally, Inc.

1903. The Gillette Razor Blade.

It took ages for civilization to hit on the idea you see below.
A flexible, disposable, affordable razor blade.
But soon (civilization being the pushy sort of thing it is), questions started popping up:
Why stop here?
Why not roll, say, 6 of these blades into a *band?*
Why not seal this band in a little cartridge, so you never have to touch its edge?
Why not put a lever on the razor, to unwind the band as you need it?
Why not indeed?

1965. The Gillette Razor Band.

The band idea is the basis of our new Techmatic Razor.

It replaces the whole blade-changing routine.

Gillette, however, does not judge a razor by how handy it is. We judge it by how well it shaves.

There is a light feel to this shave, a sheer comfort about it that cannot be compared to anything else in shaving.

There is also much less chance of a nick.

We believe the Razor Band is here to stay.

Though in another age or two, civilization may hit on a better idea.

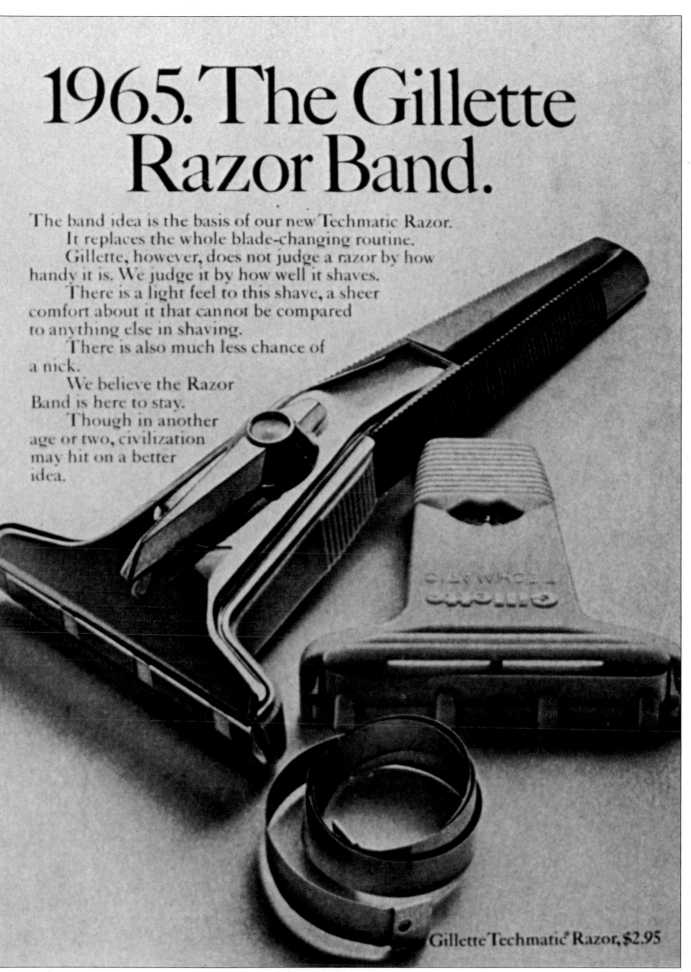

Gillette Techmatic® Razor, $2.95

Jack Tinker & Partners, Inc.

Alka-Seltzer. For People in Love.

You've all been there before. You know the feeling. You can't eat. You can't sleep. You can't think.

With Alka-Seltzer, though, you can weather the storm.

With Alka-Seltzer by your side, you can relieve a love-sick stomach, a tension headache, a foolish heartburn, and spring fever.

When it isn't even spring.

MILES LABORATORIES, INC., Consumer Products Division

All during the sixties, regardless of the agency involved, Alka-Seltzer strategy remained consistent. Their approach was to make light of stomach distress—to sell with humor. This ad and the following two commercials by Jack Tinker & Partners are some classic examples of that approach.

STOMACH: Did you ever think of me once? Once in my life?

MAN: (Unintelligible—talking at same time as stomach)

VOICE OVER: Control yourself. You say one thing. Your stomach says another.

MAN: We don't get along. Heaven knows I've tried.

STOMACH: Sure. He's tried. He gave up hot tamales. Now he's on a new kick. Pepperoni pizzas. And I was just getting used to hot tamales.

MAN: I like pepperoni pizzas.
STOMACH: Do you like heart burn? Well, you're gonna get it every time you eat a pepperoni pizza.

STOMACH: And the way he stuffs himself at his mother's.
MAN: You've always hated my mother.

STOMACH: Are you going to start that business all over again?

VOICE OVER: This isn't going to get us anywhere. You can't expect him to give up the food he loves. Man does not live by bread alone.
STOMACH: Oh please.

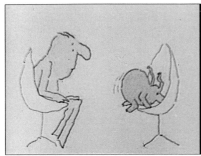

VOICE OVER: And you. When you eat spicy foods—help your stomach out. Alka-Seltzer has alkalizers which will calm your upset stomach.

It even has a pain reliever for your head.
STOMACH: Ah. Listen. That's not my department.

VOICE OVER: You take care of him. He won't bother you.
MAN: Well. I'll try ... if you will.

Jack Tinker & Partners, Inc.

VOICE OVER: Get set!

FIRST MAN: That was pretty good
pie for a change. What was it?
Blueberry pie?

SECOND MAN: Yeah. Blueberry.
First contest, kid? Follow me.

This is Alka-Seltzer.
Gets rid of that stuffy feeling.

When you've been on the circuit
as long as I have, you'll know.

See you around, kid.

VOICE OVER: Next time you overeat,
take what the guys who overeat
for a living take—Alka-Seltzer.

Jack Tinker & Partners, Inc.

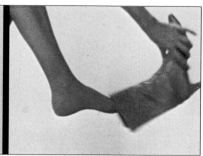

VOICE OVER: When a Braniff
International hostess meets you on
the airplane she'll be dressed
like this.

When she brings you
your dinner she'll be dressed
this way.

After dinner on those
long flights she'll slip into something
a little more comfortable.

The air strip is brought to you   who believes that even an airline
by Braniff International,   hostess should look like a girl.

Product parity—or a plane is a plane is a plane—has always been a fact of life in the airline industry. That's why
airlines and their ad agencies continually engage in aggressive promotions that seek to establish points of difference between one carrier and another. Today, the battle is waged over such prosaic matters as ticket prices, flight
schedules, punctuality and the comparative levels of discomfort to which passengers will submit.

Ah, but it was not always thus. In the exuberant and relatively innocent sixties—before stewardesses organized
for longevity and feminists expressed appropriate outrage—airlines lured jaded businessmen with more exotic
appeals. One of the most memorable and effective of these was "The Air Strip," created by Mary Wells for client
Braniff International. It captured imagination and share of market.

Who knows? Maybe they really were the good old days.

Chantilly from the House of Houbigant. Perfume imported from France, 1 oz. at $22.50 an

There is enough
Chantilly
in this
innocent pink spray

to shake
your world.

Eau de Toilette Spray Mist from $4.00, Dusting Powder from $3.00, Eau de Toilette from $3.75, Body Powder Mist $3.75, Perfume Oil $3.75, compounded in U.S.A.

Photographer Harold Becker, working with Joe Nissen's design and Ed Hanft's copy (another creative team that ended up owning the shop), took this remarkable shot in 1966. The craft and the artistry of the creative revolution were well defined by them, as this beautiful marriage of art and copy attests. This ad communicated on another (and higher) level. It almost defied its readers not to try the product.

JINGLE

BREAKING
THE
BARRIERS

4 Nobody called them "ethnics" back in the sixties, but that's what they were. Italians, Jews, Greeks, Irish: tough, cocky and very talented kids straight from the streets of the big cities. They graduated from plebeian centers of learning with undistinguished names like City College and Brooklyn College and Pratt Institute. At any other point in time, these "ethnics" of the sixties—first or second generation Americans for the most part—would have had next to no chance at all of breaking into the tight little world of advertising. A decade before, the best-selling novel and hit movie, *Gentleman's Agreement,* had documented and spotlighted the ugly, unwritten rules which governed the business.

Like banking, publishing, the stock market, or any other stylish enterprise, advertising was almost totally dominated by the Eastern establishment. The most important credentials anyone could bring to a job interview were an Ivy League education, a Protestant affiliation and a white skin—all of which, in one way or another, were expected to lead to an influential connection with one or more members of the "old boy network."

The advertising business was a country club stronghold, but against it, an urban assault was being mounted.

What novels, movies, protests, and legal arguments could not undo, the creative revolution did. A half-century of discriminatory employment practices—a virtual wall of bigotry and prejudice—was crumbling under a battering ram of talent. To compete effectively and successfully in the sixties, advertising agencies suddenly were faced with the need to recruit a new kind of employee with nontraditional attitudes and unconventional notions. Where could talent like that be found? Where was it developed? Mainly, in the streets and schools of New York City, with an occasional assist from Chicago and points West.

New business, or rather the desire to acquire it, led the agencies to seek out talent. Nothing else counted for much with advertisers. Agencies weren't awarded any points, or clients, for showing offices full of grey-flanneled account managers. Blue jeans were in, and only the new creative types wore them.

When advertisers recognized that superior creative effort could result in increased sales and share of market, agencies began to beef up their investment in creative personnel, without regard to old school ties or ethnic origins. With millions of dollars at stake, Ivy League connections became insignificant when compared to ability. At most agencies, power started to shift from account managers to creative directors; at the very least, it

was shared. Art directors and copywriters began to move into the executive suites of established agencies, as well as striking out on their own, successfully.

These were significant changes in the traditional positions of power within the agency structure. They often led to conflict and personality clashes within many shops. Talent was on the move. New agencies were being formed at an extraordinary rate, and creative skills were in great demand.

Every time a new agency opened for business in the sixties, it meant more opportunity—without discrimination—for copywriters and art directors. Many of the start-ups were by "ethnics"—minority group members—so there was little point in establishment shops continuing their restrictive employment practices. Discrimination wouldn't keep the Italians and Jews and others out of the business, but it might keep needed talent from applying for jobs that needed filling.

The growing importance of "ethnic" art directors, and their impact on the business, was amusingly evidenced in 1964. Wide World Photos, an international news and stock photography service, placed an ad in an industry trade magazine, *Advertising Age.* Under the heading, "Are Italian Art Directors More Creative?", they published a photograph of sixteen successful art directors. Naturally, all of them Italian. Three worked for old-line Madison Avenue agencies, a clear indication that old barriers were being chipped away; two worked for the *New York Herald-Tribune,* a daily newspaper much praised and honored for its good taste and contemporary approach to graphic design; while the remaining nine, an unsurprising number, all worked for agencies that had been in business

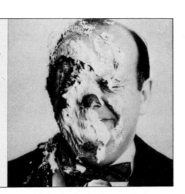

You don't think restaurants get the money to pay for fancy decor out of the air, do you?
No. They get it out of their beef.

If a restaurant gives you "atmosphere," you either have to pay through the nose for it, or the money to pay for it has to come out of the food. In which case you pay through the mouth.

Horn & Hardart saves a lot of money by not buying gaudy things you can't eat. We put what we save into our food.

Try Horn & Hardart. But keep one thing in mind. You go to a good restaurant for good food. If you want something nice to look at, try looking at your plate.

We can afford to serve meaty hamburgers instead of fatty ones.

We can afford to pay an extra 10¢ a pound for Choice grade roast beef instead of Good or Standard grades. We can afford to use Choice or Prime grade beef in our pot pies and stews instead of Utility or Commercial grades.

Horn & Hardart. It's not fancy. But it's good.

"It's not fancy. But it's good." That's the slogan created by copywriter Ed McCabe, then at the Carl Ally agency, for client Horn & Hardart. It also describes the campaign. The copy hammers at the same thought like a series of jabs. Ron Barrett's layouts are not fancy, either, just good. These are ads that could only have been conceived by a creative team and an agency that was wise to big city ways, that understood how to talk to a blue-collar crowd, and that knew what it meant to survive by eating for nickels and dimes. No genteel, well-heeled, Ivy League copywriter could have faked it. Automats were located in concrete canyons, not suburban malls. But they were in trouble, relics of an earlier age. They desperately needed new customers. This outspoken, tough-sounding, street-smart campaign bought them some time—with the ads seeing double and triple duty as point-of-sale and window displays.

for less than five years—or only since the start of the sixties.

This was further evidence of the number of job opportunities being provided by new agencies. The creative revolution was dramatically reshaping the ad business, opening it up to new people and new agencies.

One month later, Wide World Photos was at it again, this time with a fabricated and humorous plea for equal attention by an equal number of Jewish art directors. Three were employed by McCann-Erickson, a huge agency that was led unconventionally by Marion Harper.

Of the thirteen remaining Jewish art directors identified in the ad, two were at Doyle Dane Bernbach and another two at Grey Advertising (no surprise in either instance); one worked for a movie studio and one for CBS; the final seven were all employed by agencies that hadn't even existed when the sixties got underway.

Most of the young art directors in those two 1964 ads—there were few older Italian and Jewish art directors around in those days—have names that would be familiar to most people in the business today. In fact, it's as if these men and women had been elected "most likely to succeed" in the class of '64. In almost no time at all, many of them went on to become partners and principals of their own important new agencies.

After breaking into the business and beating down the ethnic barriers, it appears obvious that these Italian and Jewish art directors and copywriters did not completely trust the system to operate impartially. They must have experienced considerable doubt as to how far and how quickly they would be permitted to climb. Breaking in was one thing; taking over was quite another. From their point of view, it must have seemed less of a risk at the time to try it on their own than to stick with a company still dominated by a "WASP" mentality, no matter how quickly that mentality seemed to be changing.

Dick Jackson, a Wells, Rich, Greene creative director of the sixties and later a partner in his own successful shop, Calderhead and Jackson, recalls one of his very first job interviews. It took place following Jackson's graduation from New York's City College, an institution best known in the sixties for superior scholarship and championship basketball teams.

"I can't hire you from City College," he was told, "with just a B.A. degree. You need a Master's, at least, to work here as a writer. If

you'd come from the Ivy League, I'd put you on. But there's no chance, so forget it."

Jackson continues, "I collected my things off his desk and told him I didn't want to work for him, because I'd never let him work for me. And that was before I'd landed my first job in advertising."

Brash? Cocky? Of course! But Jackson's confidence was not misplaced or unusual for the times. Whether in sports or politics—or advertising—it's impossible to overestimate the importance of being in the right place at the right time. Call it accident, or fate, or luck, but the big city street-wise "ethnics" emerged from art school and the mail room just as the rest of America was ready to establish a dialogue with them.

These young new ethnic creative teams didn't need researchers, or interpreters, or observers to tell them what was happening. They were happening! What they designed and what they wrote and what they photographed was instinctively in step with the rest of America. It was real, it was natural, it was believable. And that made all the difference. By being themselves—something other than the establishment—they helped make the creative revolution possible. And the importance of that cannot be overestimated, either; those qualities are still prized in the most admired and successful advertising of today.

Overcoming the discrimination of elitism, snobbery and ethnic labeling were only some of the handicaps faced in the sixties by the tough kids from the streets of New York. They did it, so emphatically, that dozens of agencies bearing their Italian, Jewish, Greek and Irish names are among the biggest and most powerful in the industry today.

VOICE OVER: It doesn't take a lot of money to buy a 1970 Ambassador. It just looks like it does.

CHILD: Hey Ma! Pa! Joey's got a new car!
FATHER: Boy, Joey, that's great!

FATHER: How d'ya like the big shot? Coupla years out of college and he's bought expensive cars.

MOTHER: Joey, you need such an expensive car?
FATHER: CPAs make money. (LAUGHTER)

JOEY: Ma, Pa. It didn't cost so much. Hey! Hey Richie. Get the sneakers off the seats will ya please?
CHILD: Pa, it's got air conditioning.

MOTHER: Joey, so fancy!
JOEY: Ma. The Ambassador comes that way. Hey, come on. Let's go for a ride huh?

MOTHER: Joey! The way I'm dressed?

JOEY: You look beautiful.

MAN: BRAVO—Joe.

MOTHER: Hey Mrs. DeVoto. My son is air conditioned.

OLD WOMAN: That's nice.

VOICE OVER: The Ambassador is still the only car in its class with standard air conditioning. That's class.

If ever a new shop was "hot," that shop was Wells, Rich, Greene. New clients kept falling in, among them American Motors Corporation. AMC was not your typical Detroit auto account. They were poor relations from the wrong side of the tracks.

Then again, WRG was not your typical advertising agency. For struggling AMC they produced a series of extremely funny and highly original commercials that were totally different from all other auto commercials being aired. "Little Italy," shown here, was noteworthy not only for its New York, streetwise humor and Howard Zieff's brilliant direction, but also for Robert DeNiro's appearance in the starring role.

DeNiro is but one of many famous Hollywood actors who paid their first bills with checks from ad agencies.

71

No. 2 says he tries harder.

Than who?

We wouldn't, for a minute, argue with No. 2. If he says he tries harder, we'll take him at his word.

The only thing is, a lot of people assume it's us he's trying harder than.

That's hardly the case. And we're sure that No. 2 would be the first to agree.

Especially in light of the following.

A car where you need it.

The first step in renting a car is getting to the car. Hertz makes that easier for you to do than anybody else.

We're at every major airport in the United States. And at some airports that are not so major. Ever fly to Whitefish, Montana? Some people do. And have a Hertz car waiting.

No matter how small the airport you fly to, if it's served by a commercial airline, 97 chances out of 100 it's also served by Hertz or by a Hertz office within 20 minutes of it.

In all, Hertz has over 2,900 places throughout the world where you can pick up or leave a car. Nearly twice as many as No. 2.

Can't come to us? We'll come to you.

We have a direct-line telephone in most major hotels and motels in the U.S. It's marked HERTZ and it's in the lobby. Pick it up, ask for a car, and we'll deliver one to the door. You often can't get a cab as easily.

What kind of car would you like?

When you rent from Hertz, you're less likely to get stuck with a beige sedan when you want a red convertible. We have over twice as many cars as No. 2.

Not only is our fleet big, it's varied. We do our best to give you what you want. From Fords, to Mustangs, to Thunderbirds, to Lincolns and everything in between. Including the rather fantastic Shelby GT 350-H.

Who's perfect?

When you rent a new car from us or anybody else, you expect it to be sitting there waiting, ready to go, looking like new.

On that score we claim no superiority over our competition. They goof once in awhile. We goof once in awhile.

Except when we goof it bothers us more because people don't expect the big one to goof. And to make up for it, if our service is not up to Hertz standards we give you $50 in free rentals.* Plus an apology.

No. 2 gives a quarter plus an apology. And advertises that he "can't afford" to do more.

We feel the other way about it. We can't afford to do less.

Besides, the $50 comes out of the station manager's local operating funds. This tends to keep him very alert...and our service very good.

Hot line.

When you're in one city and you're flying to another city and you want to have a car waiting when you arrive and you want it confirmed before you leave, we can do it for you. Instantly. In any one of 1,038 U.S. cities. No other rent a car company can make that statement.

The major reason we can do it is because we recently installed one of the world's most advanced reservations systems.

After all, with the supersonic jets in sight and one hour coast to coast flights in prospect, you'll need some quick answers.

We can give them to you today.

About credit.

If you've got a national credit card with most any major company, you've got credit with us.

About rates.

You can rent a car from Hertz by the day and the mile, by the weekend, by the week, by the month, by gift certificate, by revolving credit, by sundry other ways in between.

We offer all these rates for two reasons. To stay ahead of competition. To get more people to rent cars.

When you go to rent a Hertz car just tell the Hertz girl how long you want the car and roughly how much driving you'll be doing. She'll figure out the rate that's cheapest for you.

Speak up No. 3.

Is it you that No. 2 tries harder than?

*There's one thing you have to do for us: fill out our Certified Service form and mail it to our main office in its self-addressed envelope. Upon verification we'll send you $50 in rental certificates by return mail.

©Hertz System, Inc., 1966

Hertz

For about six years, the Avis advertising campaign took dead aim at Hertz, without any effective counterpunch ever being thrown by number one. Finally, Hertz found Carl Ally. It was one of those rare occasions in the ad business when strategy dictated that you sell more than your own product or service. For employee morale, company pride and public perception, the situation demanded a telling response to a goading

One such memorable
a radio campaign in New
brand of herring called Vit
"The Herring Maven" to th
word meaning know-it-all
expert when it came to he
limited campaign that it b
than radio. Vita won conve
maven became part of the

competitor who was riding off with your customers and your dignity. Hertz
finally did it. Their new campaign came out swinging and transformed a
one-sided argument into an old-fashioned street brawl. Jim Durfee's caustic
copy demolished the Avis platform. After the appearance of these ads, the
Avis campaign never again attained the same level of intensity and success
that it had enjoyed previously.

HUSBAND: My whole family's waiting out there—
my Uncle Giuseppe, Aunt Rosa, Cousin Paolo, Momma, Papa.
What does Sophie know about cooking Italian?

She's a Polish girl from Cleveland. And the first
time my family comes to dinner she cooks
chicken cacciatore.

WIFE: Who says you have to be Italian to cook like one?

WOMAN: Good chicken!

WIFE: I got the stuff from Morelli. Fryers, spices,
wine, and I got Hunt's tomato paste too. See how
rich and thick it is?
HUSBAND: Hunt's?

MAN: Good chicken cacciatore!

VOICE OVER: With rich, thick Hunt's tomato paste
on your side, you don't have to be Italian
to cook like one.

It would be impossible to count the number of imitations spawned by this teary and touching (and funny!) commercial for Hunt's tomato sauce. You know the scene: nice Polish girl (substitute Irish, Jewish, etc.) marries Italian boy. The big test comes when his family is invited to dinner for the first time. Naturally, the Polish bride is expected to prepare—flawlessly—a traditional Italian meal. The young couple is extremely nervous, because "mama" is going to be a very tough critic. He is not wholly supportive, because the tomato sauce—so critical to the success of the whole venture—has not been made from scratch. For shame! She got it from a can—a can of Hunt's. Mama tastes. Mama pauses. Mama nods. And mama smiles. Family laughs. Husband beams—he never had a doubt. What a triumph! It's a marriage made in heaven, or a Hunt's tomato sauce can. It's the kind of authentic American corn that U.S. agencies have been turning out for the past twenty-five years. But this was special, because it was the first of a genre.

TEN
YEARS:
TEN
LANDMARK
CAMPAIGNS

5

During the sixties, hundreds of great ads were created each year by dozens of advertising agencies practicing the "new creativity." Many creative teams found the magic on more than one occasion, and produced individual ads of exceptional creative merit. But it remained difficult to pull a great campaign out of the hat.

Brilliance was most often displayed in occasional flashes. A consistent fire—the kind of conceptual thinking required for an entire advertising campaign—was not so easily generated.

For example, David Ogilvy wrote a great ad for Rolls-Royce automobiles, but there was no great Rolls-Royce campaign that followed. In 1962, Benton & Bowles created an extraordinary ad for Western Union telegrams, but there was no extraordinary Western Union campaign backing it up. Early in the sixties, George Lois and Julian Koenig produced a series of superb ads introducing Wolfschmidt vodka —but even two or three classic efforts do not make a great campaign.

A great advertising campaign imparts a special quality, an intangible but important extra value to the product being advertised. The ads become more than effective sales tools, they become an extension of the product itself. In fact, a great campaign not only sells the product, it sells itself.

With advertisers seeking new approaches and agencies encouraged to take some risks, virtually all advertising strained to attain creative levels higher than those which had been reached before. Successful development and execution of a campaign concept was the ultimate creative achievement. If it's a challenge to produce just one ad that qualifies for greatness, imagine the degree of difficulty, energy and ingenuity required to mount and sustain a long-term campaign. The concepts, the creative consistency, the execution—all the elusive elements required to produce a great campaign—came together in the sixties with greater frequency than ever before, or since. It can be truthfully claimed that more memorable advertising surfaced in the sixties than in the fifties and seventies combined. In both of those decades it's difficult to recall ten advertising campaigns that qualified for greatness.

What made the sixties so much fun and so exciting is the fact that recalling ten great campaigns is comparatively easy. The difficulty is in confining our choice to just ten.

Nevertheless, we have managed to select ten campaigns which we believe were the best and most memorable of the era, the campaigns whose influence can clearly be seen today.

Volkswagen *For anyone connected in any way with the business of advertising, there probably won't be much argument about our choice of the Volkswagen campaign as the very best of the sixties. Indeed, if the sixties were the best of creative times, then the Volkswagen campaign is not merely the best of the sixties, but the best of all time.*

There are many reasons to believe this. First, the Volkswagen creative strategy was so solid that any number of talented DDB copywriters were able to write brilliantly for the campaign. Even experienced observers would be hard-pressed to identify any individual styles or characteristics in the hundreds of ads and commercials that sold the "Beetle" or the "Bug" to America. The art direction was so stunningly and deceptively simple that, at one time, readers were even asked to create their own Volkswagen ads.

Volkswagen had a larger budget than the other sixties advertisers with the most memorable campaigns—and so Volkswagen advertising was by far the most diverse. Just another of the many reasons for making it our number one choice.

Volkswagen's irresistible, irreverent and indelible messages appeared in print, on television, on posters, and on the radio with unflagging energy and wit. And the marvel is that they did so year after year without ever appearing tired, shopworn, repetitive—and without ever wearing out their welcome. The car ran out of gas before the campaign.

Lemon.

This Volkswagen missed the boat.

The chrome strip on the glove compartment is blemished and must be replaced. Chances are you wouldn't have noticed it; Inspector Kurt Kroner did.

There are 3,389 men at our Wolfsburg factory with only one job: to inspect Volkswagens at each stage of production. (3000 Volkswagens are produced daily; there are more inspectors than cars.)

Every shock absorber is tested (spot checking won't do), every windshield is scanned. VWs have been rejected for surface scratches barely visible to the eye.

Final inspection is really something! VW inspectors run each car off the line onto the Funktionsprüfstand (car test stand), tote up 189 check points, gun ahead to the automatic brake stand, and say "no" to one VW out of fifty.

This preoccupation with detail means the VW lasts longer and requires less maintenance, by and large, than other cars. (It also means a used VW depreciates less than any other car.)

We pluck the lemons; you get the plums.

TEN
YEARS:
TEN
LANDMARK
CAMPAIGNS

VOLKSWAGEN

© VOLKSWAGEN OF AMERICA, INC.

We finally came up with a beautiful picture of a Volkswagen.

A Volkswagen starts looking good when everything else starts looking bad.

Let's say it's late at night and you can't sleep. It's 10 below and you forgot to put antifreeze in your car.

(A Volkswagen doesn't use antifreeze. Its engine is cooled by air.)

Let's say it's now morning: You start your car and the gas gauge reads Empty.

(Even with a gallon left, you should go approximately 27 miles in a VW.)

Let's say you notice on your way out of the driveway that every other car on your block is stuck in the snow.

(A VW goes very well in snow because the engine is in the back. It gives the rear wheels much better traction.)

Let's say you make it into town and the only parking space is half a space between a snow plow and a big, fat wall.

(A VW is small enough to fit into half a parking space.)

Let's say it's now 9:15 a.m. and the only other guy in the office is your boss.

(Now what could be more beautiful than that?)

"It was the only thing to do after the mule died."

Three years back, the Hinsleys of Dora, Missouri, had a tough decision to make.

To buy a new mule.

Or invest in a used bug.

They weighed the two possibilities.

First there was the problem of the bitter Ozark winters. Tough on a warm-blooded mule. Not so tough on an air-cooled VW.

Then, what about the eating habits of the two contenders? Hay vs. gasoline.

As Mr. Hinsley puts it: "I get over eighty miles out of a dollar's worth of gas and I get where I want to go a lot quicker."

Then there's the road leading to their cabin. Many a mule pulling a wagon and many a conventional automobile has spent many an hour stuck in the mud.

As for shelter, a mule needs a barn. A bug doesn't. "It just sets out there all day and the paint job looks near as good as the day we got it."

Finally, there was maintenance to think about. When a mule breaks down, there's only one thing to do: Shoot it.

But if and when their bug breaks down, the Hinsleys have a Volkswagen dealer only two gallons away.

TEN
YEARS:
TEN
LANDMARK
CAMPAIGNS

VOLKSWAGEN

Some shapes are hard to improve on.

Ask any hen.

You just can't design a more functional shape for an egg.

And we figure the same is true of the Volkswagen Sedan.

Don't think we haven't tried.

(As a matter of fact, the Volkswagen's been changed nearly 3,000 times.)

But we can't improve our basic design.

Like the egg, it's the right kind of package for what goes inside.

So that's where most of our energy goes.

To get more power without using more gas. To put synchromesh on first gear. To improve the heater. That kind of thing.

As a result, our package carries four adults, and their luggage, at about 32 miles to a gallon of regular gas and 40,000 miles to a set of tires.

 We've made a few external changes, of course. Such as push-button doorknobs.

Which is one up on the egg.

In 1949 we sold 2 Volkswagens in the U.S.A.

What a kidding the owners of those two Volkswagens must have taken.

But they had something to sustain them.

32 miles to the gallon. An engine in the rear that carried them (and their stranded neighbors) up icy hills. An air-cooled engine that never boiled over or froze.

They fiercely defended the beetle shape against a thousand jokes, and saw it become a beloved classic.

And finally, they had the sweet satisfaction of seeing one kidder after another turn up with a new Volkswagen of his own!

We think our two '49ers would get a kick out of knowing how many Americans bought a Volkswagen in 1960. Around 185,000 (including station wagons and trucks.) That's 23% more than in '59.

And if they still own those 12 year old VWs, they can drive into any Volkswagen dealer in any part of the U. S. and find replacement parts on hand.

The Volkswagen is still basically the same. But *people* have changed.

TEN
YEARS:
TEN
LANDMARK
CAMPAIGNS

VOLKSWAGEN

VOICE OVER: Have you ever wondered   how the man who drives a snow plow

drives to the snow plow?   This one drives a Volkswagen.   So you can stop wondering.

TEN
YEARS:
TEN
LANDMARK
CAMPAIGNS

VOLKSWAGEN

VOICE OVER: I, Maxwell E. Snaberly, being of sound mind and body, do hereby bequeath the following:

to my wife Rose, who spent money like there was no tomorrow, I leave one hundred dollars and a calendar.

To my sons Rodney and Victor,

who's only motto was spend, spend, spend I leave nothing, nothing, nothing.

And to my other friends and relatives who also never learned the value of a dollar I leave a dollar.

Finally to my nephew Harold,

who spent every dime I ever gave them

on fancy cars and fast women,
I leave fifty dollars in dimes.

To my business partner Jules

who ofttimes said, "A penny saved
is a penny earned,"

and who also ofttimes said,
"Gee Uncle Max, it sure pays to own
a Volkswagen,"

I leave my entire fortune of
one hundred billion dollars.

TEN
YEARS:
TEN
LANDMARK
CAMPAIGNS

VOLKSWAGEN

VOICE OVER: Mr. Jones and Mr. Krempler were neighbors.

They each had three thousand dollars.

With his money, Mr. Jones bought himself a three thousand-dollar car.

a new washer,

a new dryer,

a record player,

th his money,

Mr. Krempler bought himself a new
refrigerator,

a new range,

o new television sets,

and a brand new Volkswagen.

Now Mr. Jones is faced with that age-old
problem: keeping up with the Kremplers.

TEN
YEARS:
TEN
LANDMARK
CAMPAIGNS

AVIS

Avis Avis had not been traveling in the fast lane. It was a company with an almost unbroken record of failure and financial losses for nearly fifteen years. The entire organization needed repairs and new parts. The first major overhaul occurred in 1962, with the appointment of Robert Townsend as chief executive. This was followed almost immediately by assigning the advertising to Doyle Dane Bernbach. Avis was getting ready to shift into high gear.

In 1963—almost overnight—Avis raced into the black, propelled by advertising. In some ways the Avis campaign was an even more daring breakthrough than the advertising DDB was doing for Volkswagen. Nobody could recall any other advertising like it. Imagine a company actually admitting it was only number two in its industry. Research indicated that the campaign should not run, and if it did, it would fail. So much for research, at least as practiced in the sixties.

But there was more to the Avis creative strategy than a catchy headline. The ads appealed to every struggling underdog (that's most of us) to strike a financial blow against a smug, swaggering top dog. When you cut through the veneer of this ingenious campaign, what surfaced was a rough, hard-hitting approach that hammered away at Hertz. Although cleverly masked, the Avis campaign

was another of the many scrappy, street-smart concepts that marked so much of the successful advertising of the sixties.

The ad layouts were truly unusual, dominated by typography instead of photography or illustration. If there had been a larger budget available, if a major effort in media other than print had been sustained, and if it had enjoyed a little longer run, in our opinion the Avis campaign might very well have challenged the Volkswagen campaign as the best of all time. It not only turned the advertiser's fortunes around instantly, but it also transformed Avis into a popular underdog, with everyone rooting for them to succeed.

Here are Paula Green's written recollections about the campaign she created with art director Helmut Krone:

"It almost didn't run.
Everything was against it.
It was a thorny ad.
It wasn't pretty, it printed unprintable truths, it exposed the naked company to the public.
It made a lot of people uncomfortable.
It even irritated a lot of people here.
It researched miserably.
Bill Bernbach had the courage to sell it.
The client had the courage to buy it.
It is a one-page summary of Doyle Dane Bernbach."

Would you like to send an Avis button to your son at college?

We try harder.

Or to the man who installed your dishwasher? Or to the laundry that doesn't replace the buttons on your shirts?

It might wake up somebody you know. The way it did us.

The button jacked us up. It reminded us we were only No. 2 in rent a cars. With a lot more to do than just hand you a car like a lively new Ford.

We had to try harder to keep you coming back. All of us.

The girls at the counters, the men who fill up the gas tanks, the mechanics, the president back at the office. We're still only No. 2. But we're inching up.

Pick up a button at any Avis counter.

If the slogan doesn't work, turn it over.

Try the pin.

Avis is only No.2 in rent a cars. So why go with us?

We try harder.

(When you're not the biggest, you have to.)

We just can't afford dirty ash-trays. Or half-empty gas tanks. Or worn wipers. Or unwashed cars. Or low tires. Or anything less than seat–adjusters that adjust. Heaters that heat. Defrosters that defrost.

Obviously, the thing we try hardest for is just to be nice. To start you out right with a new car, like a lively, super-torque Ford, and a pleasant smile. To know, say, where you get a good pastrami sandwich in Duluth.

Why?

Because we can't afford to take you for granted.

Go with us next time.

The line at our counter is shorter.

TEN
YEARS:
TEN
LANDMARK
CAMPAIGNS

AVIS

Avis can't afford dirty ashtrays.

Or to start you out without a full gas tank, a new car like a lively, super-torque Ford, a smile.

Why?

When you're not the biggest in rent a cars, you have to try harder.

We do.

We're only No. 2.

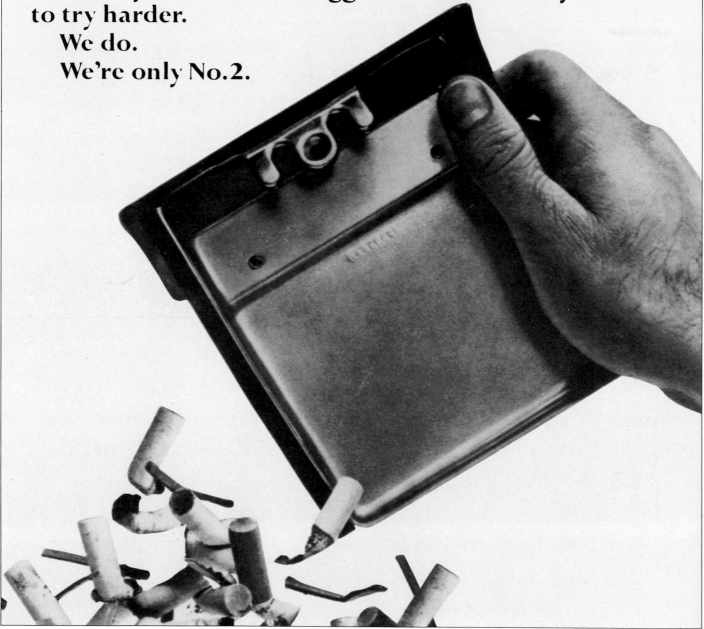

No. 2ism.
The Avis Manifesto.

We are in the rent a car business, playing second fiddle to a giant.

Above all, we've had to learn how to stay alive.

In the struggle, we've also learned the basic difference between the No.1's and No.2's of the world.

The No.1 attitude is: "Don't do the wrong thing. Don't make mistakes and you'll be O.K."

The No.2 attitude is: "Do the right thing. Look for new ways. Try harder."

No.2ism is the Avis doctrine. And it works.

The Avis customer rents a clean, new Plymouth, with wipers wiping, ashtrays empty, gas tank full, from an Avis girl with smile firmly in place.

And Avis itself has come out of the red into the black.

Avis didn't invent No.2ism. Anyone is free to use it.

No.2's of the world, arise!

TEN
YEARS:
TEN
LANDMARK
CAMPAIGNS

AVIS

Are you working like a dog to get to the top? Shake hands with Avis.

Welcome to the club.

When you're not top dog, you try harder. You work more hours. You worry more. You eat much too fast.

You go through the same thing Avis is going through. We're only No. 2 in rent a cars.

We have to knock ourselves out to please people.

By not giving them anything less than fine cars like lively super-torque Fords. By worrying that one of our people might forget to empty an ashtray. Or clean a windshield. Or fill a gas tank. We try harder. But you'll never know how hard we try until you try us.

Walk up to our counter.

And give us some growing pains to keep our stomach pains company.

© 1964 AVIS, INC.

The writer of this ad rented an Avis car recently. Here's what I found:

Cigarette butts. A whole ashtray full.

I write Avis ads for a living. But that doesn't make me a paid liar.

When I promise that the least you'll get from Avis is a clean Plymouth with everything in perfect order, I expect Avis to back me up.

I don't expect full ashtrays; it's not like them.

I know for a fact that everybody in that company, from the president down, tries harder.

"We try harder" was their idea; not mine.

And now they're stuck with it; not me.

So if I'm going to continue writing these ads, Avis had better live up to them. Or they can get themselves a new boy.

They'll probably never run this ad.

TEN
YEARS:
TEN
LANDMARK
CAMPAIGNS

AVIS

Avis can't afford unwashed cars.

Or smudged mirrors, dirty ashtrays, or anything less than new cars like lively, super-torque Fords.
Why?
When you're not the biggest in rent a cars, you have to try harder.
We do.
We're only No. 2.

© 1963 AVIS, INC.

SON: When my father rented a Plymouth from Avis he got these bug stickers to use if they goofed up somewheres.

If Avis thinks that's how to get ahead that's okay by me.

What gripes me is, Dad uses the stickers at home. FATHER (OVER): If it works for Avis, why not the whole country?

VOICE OVER: If you get a rent a car with a burned-out headlight blame it on the one-eyed car bug.

We're keeping our eyes peeled for him at Avis. We can't expect you to keep renting our shiny

new Plymouths if we don't keep out the bugs.

ANNOUNCER: Avis is only number two, but we don't want you to rent our Plymouth because you feel sorry for us.

If our cars aren't any cleaner, if the service at our counter isn't any faster, let Avis die.

America doesn't need another mediocre company.

Three 10-second spots

TEN
YEARS:
TEN
LANDMARK
CAMPAIGNS

LEVY'S

Levy's *Throughout the sixties Doyle Dane Bernbach broke the rules, proving there were no rules when it came to creating great advertising. Therefore, it is not nearly so difficult to break one of our own rules by selecting Levy's campaign as one of our top ten.*

We commented earlier that the advertising for Wolfschmidt Vodka, no matter how brilliant, was more a series than a campaign. In the same manner, Doyle Dane Bernbach's work for Levy's Jewish Rye was not much more than a series of posters—also converted into newspaper ads. But the work has been etched so sharply in memory, has survived so long and so well, copied and parodied by so many others ever since it first appeared, that the selection of this campaign as one of the best of the sixties has been made without any hesitation.

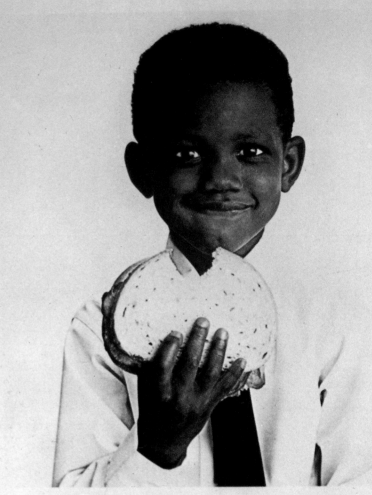

100

You don't have to be Jewish

to love Levy's
real Jewish Rye

TEN
YEARS:
TEN
LANDMARK
CAMPAIGNS

LEVY'S

You don't have to be Jewish

to love Levy's
real Jewish Rye

You don't have to be Jewish

to love Levy's
real Jewish Rye

TEN
YEARS:
TEN
LANDMARK
CAMPAIGNS

CHIVAS
REGAL

Chivas Regal Great advertising has the ability to involve the reader or viewer. Nowhere is this point better made than in the advertising DDB created for Chivas Regal. The company did not have a massive budget. It did not have category leadership. It did not have instant recognition as a premium scotch—and certainly not as <u>the</u> premium scotch. Other brands come to mind as being more solidly entrenched at that time. Certainly, Haig & Haig's Pinch Bottle was enjoying substantial success as an important premium brand. Johnnie Walker Red and Black, both of which retain their hold on important segments of the premium scotch market, also enjoyed considerable favor in the early sixties. And there were others—Cutty Sark, Dewar's, Teacher's. No scotch, however, came so far on so modest an expenditure, and achieved so much through advertising, as Chivas Regal.

On the surface, the creative strategy, like so many others developed and refined by the creative teams at DDB, appeared relatively simple: just explain why Chivas Regal was worth more money. But successful advertising, as Bill Bernbach has pointed out, does not lie in <u>what</u> you say—but in the <u>way</u> you say it. Ad after

Chivas ad, DDB writers and artists said it with headlines and photographs that captured the imagination, the respect and the affection of premium scotch buyers. From an early ad that justified a packaging change to the elevation of the brand at the very top of its category, the campaign was a tour de force, and remains so. The words and pictures differed with each new ad, but the Chivas message of quality always came through in precisely the same way.

This campaign also calls for a tip of the hat to the power of print advertising. Hard liquor, of course, cannot be advertised on television in America. The impressive results achieved by the Chivas campaign and the share of mind and market that it captured demonstrated that intelligent, charming, disarming and witty magazine advertising could produce a substantial change in consumer preferences, and carry a brand to a position of leadership.

This bottle is ½ empty.

This bottle is ½ full.

If it happens to be your bottle of Chivas that reaches the halfway mark, you'll probably feel it's half empty.

Whereas, if you're visiting a friend and his bottle reaches the same point, you can relax, knowing that it's still half full.

12 YEARS OLD WORLDWIDE · BLENDED SCOTCH WHISKY · 86 PROOF · GENERAL WINE & SPIRITS CO., NEW YORK, N.Y.

TEN
YEARS:
TEN
LANDMARK
CAMPAIGNS

CHIVAS
REGAL

Tsk, tsk.

12-YEAR-OLD BLENDED SCOTCH WHISKY · 86 PROOF
GENERAL WINE AND SPIRITS CO., NEW YORK, N.Y.

After a party, the host is often faced with several almost-empty Scotch bottles.

And there's a natural tendency to consolidate the leftovers in a single bottle.

Guess whose.

Now we don't intend to comment on the morality of this. (We're kind of flattered that the Chivas Regal bottle should so often have the honor.)

But please don't. You're not fooling anyone. Anyone who knows Scotch, that is.

Chivas Regal is a very distinctive whisky. Many people consider it the smoothest of all Scotches.

It's made with prize Glenlivet whiskies from the oldest distillery in the Scottish Highlands.

And every drop is aged 12 years.

Newcomers ask us how much training it takes to tell Chivas Regal from the others.

Order a glass at your local bar. Sip it, neat.

That should do the trick.

Go ahead.
Spend the extra $2.

It's Christmas, isn't it?

12-YEAR-OLD BLENDED SCOTCH WHISKY-86 PROOF-GENERAL WINE & SPIRITS CO., N.Y.

TEN
YEARS:
TEN
LANDMARK
CAMPAIGNS

**CHIVAS
REGAL**

Look at it this way.
You didn't lose a bottle of Chivas;
you gained a few friends.

Jamaica Tourism *Another in our top ten from Doyle Dane Bernbach is the much honored and frequently imitated campaign for the island of Jamaica. Like virtually all other great campaigns, these ads either ignored or broke all of the supposed rules of advertising.*

Here, the dominant headline contained only one word: Jamaica. No customer benefit. No promises. Nothing to lure readers, or tourists, until you traveled further into the ads. They exerted a strong appeal—people read them and reacted. Like the Avis ads, these also broke a lot of ground, all of it productive for the Jamaica Tourist Board. Working with a comparatively limited budget, DDB managed to purchase two-page advertisements in leading magazines by innovatively designing and combining black-and-white pages with full-color pages. This, in addition to the more conventional full-color one-page ads and lyrical, lovely TV commercials narrated by Jamaicans with lilting accents, all combined to give Jamaica an image among tourists that was unique.

Creatively—in both art and copy—the campaign represented a total departure from the usual and trite travel advertising that left little to choose between one possible destination and another. Instead, readers and viewers were introduced to the people (as individuals, not faceless masses), the tradition and the culture of Jamaica. In turn, this triggered a whole battery of positive responses on the part of tourists seeking the bonus of a foreign environment while enjoying the benefits of a tropical vacation. Travel advertising as personal as this had not been attempted before. It was extraordinarily effective.

© JAMAICA TOURIST BOARD

In Kingston, you can go to a theater where all the lawn's a stage. And Jamaica is all the scenery.

8:30 P.M. The stage lights come up. The scene is a garden. Trees, lush flowers. Sweet-smelling, still. Distantly, a rooster crows. Tree toads whistle.

Juliet sighs. Romeo speaks.

You listen, sitting in a comfortable chair on the clipped lawn of a rambling house off Hope Road, lost in Verona.

In Jamaica.

If Shakespeare's not your meter, however, we also have spectacles like "A Funny Thing Happened on the Way to the Forum." And concerts. Ballets. And Louise Bennett.

You haven't seen anything until you've seen 200 pounds of beautiful Louise singing, soft-shoeing, and mugging through "Money is a Funny Ting."

Any way you look at us we're theatrical.

At beach parties, we do showy things like eat fire. Or hang from the tops of palm trees by our feet. Or balance on bicycles while removing 12 shirts.

Our women are show-stoppers. Blends of China, Africa, Britain, they're dramatic *looking*, then dress in stage-y colors like red, orange, purple. Pow.

We're even melodramatic at Christmas. In addition to sweet jolly Santa, we have scary John Canoe—grotesque masked characters who dance through the streets acting crazy, waving their hands and shooing away children.

Our kids not only look forward to getting gifts for Christmas, they look forward to getting frightened, too.

For more of the drama of Jamaica, see your local travel agent or Jamaica Tourist Board in New York, San Francisco, Los Angeles, Miami, Chicago or Toronto.

TEN
YEARS:
TEN
LANDMARK
CAMPAIGNS

JAMAICA
TOURISM

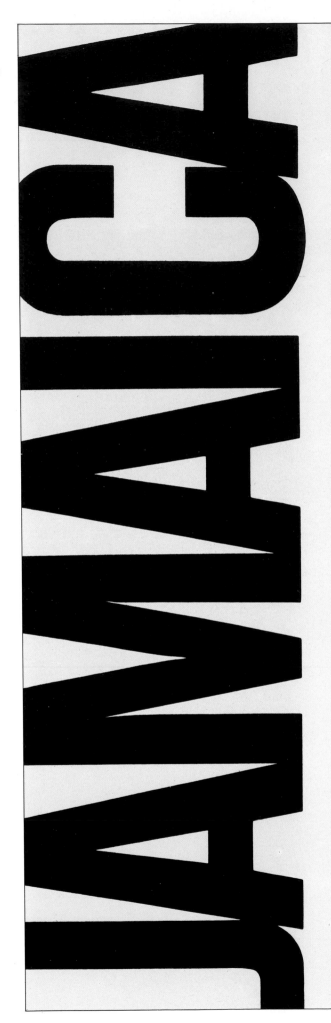

In Port Antonio, you still hear about the feats of 3 local men: Captain Bligh, Errol Flynn, and Samuel Steele.

Will Bligh had a temper.
"The trees, not the men, get the water!" he roared. So it was mutiny on the bounty. But next trip from Polynesia he brought breadfruit to Port Antonio. We've been eating it like bread since.

We owe Will a lot.

Errol Flynn had a warm temperament. Fell in love with Port Antonio. (And we with him.) Settled in with wife and daughter. (Who still skas sultry evenings at our Blue Lagoon.)

We'll never forget Errol.

Samuel Steele is a temperate man. Now. But 50 years ago, it was the Belgian trenches, Hellfire Corner, a French girl friend and 4 months' leave in Italy before returning to family life, a grocery store and yearly airings of the medals on Armistice Day.

You hear some tales from Sam.

Port Antonio has always attracted colorful men.

Dan Mitchell built a seaside castle here for his 19th century lady love, mixing the cement with sea water. Today, Mitchell's Folly is our loveliest ruin.

Dashing Ted Ruddock runs our *20th* century castle, Frenchman's Cove. Private hotel *houses*, not rooms. Champagne baths not impossible. Come with checks.

Joe Mullins, on the other hand, is "daddy" host at homey De Montevin Lodge with Mrs. Mullins in the kitchen cooking fried chicken, crackling, and coconut pie.

Come as you are.

For more of our inns (modest or lavish) and men (likewise), see your travel agent or Jamaica Tourist Board in New York, San Francisco, Los Angeles, Chicago, Miami, Toronto, Montreal.

TEN
YEARS:
TEN
LANDMARK
CAMPAIGNS

**JAMAICA
TOURISM**

JAMAICA

Spend a glorious day at the Newcastle Army Training Camp on Blue Mountain. Don't laugh. You'll have one hell of a good time.

Newcastle is one of the few army posts in the world with no AWOL problem. In fact, it's so ruddy beautiful up there, 3850 feet up Blue Mountain, with the hummingbirds dipping all around, and the Bougainvillea and honeysuckle winding over the veddy British/Colonial/Victorian buildings, and the cool, tickly hillcountry air, and the puffy clouds sailing by *under* the windows, and the 40-mile view of Kingston and the sea, and the deep gorges filled with birdsong—that the army sometimes has trouble getting the troops to leave when their training cycle's over.

We have the same problem with the civilians who visit here.

Just so you don't forget, amid all this tropical scenic splendor, that you're still on an Army post, the "management" has kindly laid out a series of mountain marches for you. (All voluntary, of course.)

Start your training easy—with a short 20-minute hike up a gentle curving path—called reassuringly, The *Ladies*' Mile. If you get your wind, you can build up to the almost vertical Catherine's Peak trip. ("Mountain goats, 25 min.; Gentlemen, 40 min.; Ladies, 55 min.; Old Soldiers and Young Children, 1 hr. 5 min.")

If Shank's Mare is not your speed, you can always rent a mule (although be forewarned: walking is faster). The mules and their masters work out of a town called Mavis Bank. To the top of the mountain and back, it's $8.40 for mon and beast. (The mon goes along to keep the beast honest.) Make an overnight trip out of it with a stay at Whitfield Hall, a rough-it hostel near the peak. $1.40 per night. It's not as plush as army life. But after all, one must make *some* sacrifices these days.

For more vacation (or enlistment) information, see your travel agent or Jamaica Tourist Board, Dept. 8N, 630 Fifth Ave., New York City 10020.

JAMAICA

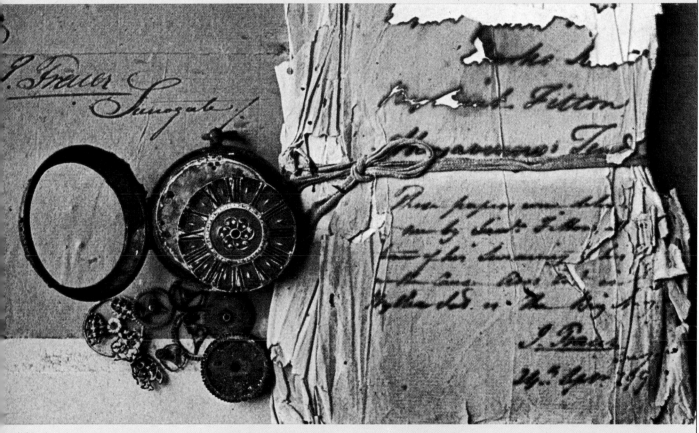

In 1692, the wicked city of Port Royal was cast into the sea. ("As retribution for her sins.") Since then, we've kept our social life a little less wild. (We're not taking any chances.)

In the midst of a bacchanalian revel on June 7, 1692, the "golden Hades" known as Port Royal disappeared quite suddenly into the sea. With all its pirate booty, bawds, ships, storehouses and written records.

Three tremors. And it was gone. (Those reverend ministers who had predicted no good for the city smiled, knowingly.)

We can't afford to lose any more cities. So please, when you come to Jamaica, take it easy. Don't spend *all* your time in wild abandon—gambling recklessly at Caymanas racetrack, dancing the frantic Ska till 4 o'clock in the morning, bargaining feverishly for the sinuous silks of the Orient along the quays, drinking the fierce 151 proof Jamaican rum in the wine shops. Spend some of your time doing *uplifting* things, too. Like visiting our museum. At the Jamaican Institute in Kingston you can see pieces of Port Royal: a few hundred artifacts, including the golden watch photographed above. Also on display is a packet of ship's papers found in the belly of a fish. (Mon, that's culture.)

When you run out of museum, there are a few other things you can do in Jamaica without getting us all tossed into the sea again. Theatre, for example. There are some marvelous little theatre groups, and a Gilbert and Sullivan company. Plus an annual Jamaican pantomime.

If you like your uplifting activities to be outdoors, you can climb a mountain. Or a waterfall. Or breathe the pungently sweet scent of a field of freshly cut sugar cane. Or listen to the chirps, cheeps, whistles and pipings of a Jamaican jungle night. (This kind of diversion may not be as much fun as the things vacationing pirates used to do here. But it's a lot safer.)

For more on Jamaica's sunken cities and raised social life, see your travel agent or Jamaica Tourist Board, Dept. 2N, 630 Fifth Ave.. New York City.

TEN
YEARS:
TEN
LANDMARK
CAMPAIGNS

**JAMAICA
TOURISM**

VOICE OVER: It has beaches.   It has mountains.   It's tranquil.

It's obvious.   It's hot.

s exciting.   It's mysterious.

s cool.   It's real life. Even though it's a dream world.   That's Jamaica.

TEN
YEARS:
TEN
LANDMARK
CAMPAIGNS

**JAMAICA
TOURISM**

(All voices have unmistakable
and musical Jamaican accents)

CHILD: Sometimes the sea is so soft,
It feels like a mattress.

(Children singing underneath)

CHILDREN: B-a-t bat!

NEXT CHILD: Dan's River Falls feels like
being in a bubble bath.

NEXT CHILD: … and it is school morning …
and the bed is soooo sweet. I don't
feel to get up to go to school.

EXT CHILD: You click your fingers.

And then you move your head and your arms and your tummy and your back.

I like when the water hits my back, it feel so tickly.

EXT CHILD: ... and sunset ...

You feel like you can go on riding forever. Just galloping away.

ANNOUNCER: For children Jamaica is kind of a paradise. But you know? Even when you grow up it's so easy to feel like a child again here.

TEN
YEARS:
TEN
LANDMARK
CAMPAIGNS

HATHAWAY

Hathaway *David Ogilvy stated frequently that humor had no place in advertising. Not for a minute did he believe that anyone ever bought anything from "clowns." So his advertising always took on the appearance and the language of a serious and intelligent salesperson —and it was filled with a lot of important little details that all contributed toward making the sale. Advertising by David Ogilvy was crafted and manufactured with perhaps even more precision than the products he was being asked to promote. He may have been opposed to light-hearted advertising, but in this classic campaign for Hathaway shirts, David Ogilvy demonstrated a quiet sense of humor that he was obviously prepared to use as a sales tool. It wasn't a belly laugh, of course, but it was a little joke of sorts. Who was Baron Wrangell? Why was he wearing an eye-patch? More important, David Ogilvy never revealed all—and that was really a bother. The answer to these questions didn't matter, but the campaign did, because the little budget behind Hathaway shirts made big waves in the marketplace. It was a high-profile campaign for both the advertiser and David Ogilvy's agency.*

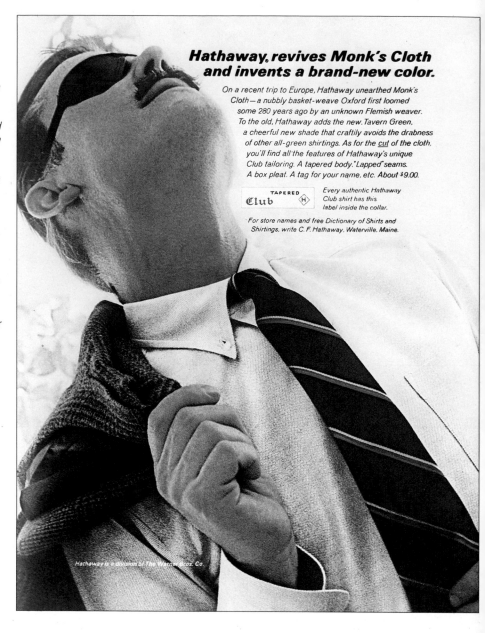

Baron Wrangell exhibits Hathaway's Loline collar. His shirt color is India Ivory. Also in Bermuda Blue and White.

Hathaway's drip-dry shirt gets an <u>air-conditioned</u> collar

FOR YEARS the textile experts have been trying to produce a drip-dry fabric that is as cool as any summer batiste. Hathaway's weavers have now succeeded.

But our cutters are not the sort of men to let a weaver walk away with all the laurels. "What's the use of a cool fabric if you don't have a cool collar?" they declared. And they went to work.

First they removed the standard thick neckband. This allows the *covered* part of your neck to breathe. You never get hot under the collar. Then they spread the points to give the collar a low sloping contour. (We call it the *Loline.*) This frees your Adam's apple and exposes more of your neck to the air.

The fabric is a precise blend of Dacron polyester fiber and fine cotton.* It drip-dries without a trace of those infernal puckers. If you're downright finicky, you *can* touch it up with an iron.

Our drip-dry shirts cost about $7.50. Other Hathaway shirts with the *Loline* collar start at $6.00. For store names, write C. F. Hathaway, Waterville, Maine. Or call OXford 7-5566 in New York.

*65% Dacron to 35% cotton. Dacron is a Du Pont trademark.

TEN
YEARS:
TEN
LANDMARK
CAMPAIGNS

HATHAWAY

Note the square-cornered cuffs on Baron Wrangell's shirt — a celebrated Hathaway hallmark.

Hathaway presents <u>Antique Ivory</u> — a color that never clashes

EVER noticed the marvelous color that ivory goes when it ages? It lies somewhere between cream and old gold. Very unobtrusive. Very soft. A perfect color for a shirt.

When Hathaway's experts were finally satisfied that an *Antique Ivory* dye could be made, we chose to present it on our famous all-cotton Batiste Oxford. You see the result above. A mellow color that refuses to clash with anything.

Hathaway pioneered Batiste Oxford many heat-waves ago. This remarkable stuff retains the look and handle of top-grade Oxford but sheds nearly half the weight. It never feels sleazy the way some summer shirtings do.

The shirt above costs about $7.50 — long or short sleeves. See the full range of Hathaway Batiste Oxfords at the better stores. They're also in White and Bermuda Blue. For store names, write C. F. Hathaway, Waterville, Maine. Call OXford 7-5566 in New York.

Shirts in Antique Ivory stripes, about $7.50; solids, about $7.

This shirt has an unusual collar. Hathaway has removed one layer of its lining — so that your neck can breathe.

Hathaway reveals the truth about men who wear drip-dry shirts

WE HAVE discovered that many men who swear by Hathaway's drip-dry shirts *never drip them dry*. They cheerfully send them to the laundry, just like any other shirt.

We asked some of these men why on earth they buy our drip-dry shirts in preference to our others. And their answers boil down to this:

After a hard day, a Hathaway drip-dry looks neater than any other shirt known to man. It is virtually crumple-proof.

Of course, if you ever wash one of these Hathaway shirts yourself, you can trust it to drip-dry looking as crisp as if you'd ironed it.

The ice-blue shirt in our picture is a summer blend of Dacron polyester fiber and cotton. It weighs a scant five ounces, and also comes in white and the subdued shades at the right: Sahara, Cactus, and Scotch Dawn. About $7.50.

Dacron is a Du Pont trademark.

For the names of stores, write to C. F. Hathaway, Waterville, Maine. Or call OXford 7-5566 in New York.

TEN
YEARS:
TEN
LANDMARK
CAMPAIGNS

HATHAWAY

Hathaway and the Duke's stud groom

IT ALL STARTED with Richard Tattersall, the Duke of Kingston's stud groom. He dressed his horses in magnificent check blankets. Then English tailors started using Mr. Tattersall's checks for gentlemen's waistcoats.

Now Hathaway takes the Tattersall one step further. With the help of an old Con-necticut mill, we have scaled down this classic pattern to miniature proportions, so that you can wear it in New York. Yet its implication of landed gentry still remains.

You can get this Hathaway miniature Tattersall in red and grey (as illustrated), navy and blue, or mahogany and beige. Between board meetings you can amuse yourself counting the various hallmarks of a Hathaway shirt: 22 single-needle stitches to the inch, big buttons, square-cut cuffs. And so forth.

The price is $8.95. For the name of your nearest store, write C. F. Hathaway, Waterville, Maine. In New York, call OXford 7-5566.

Hathaway imports Ponja cloth—from London

IN THIS PHOTOGRAPH Baron Wrangell is wearing what is probably the *lightest* shirt Hathaway ever made. So light, says the Baron, that at one point he began to wonder whether he had forgotten to put it on.

The original Ponja cloth came from India, but it is now woven in Britain. The patterns are hand-printed by the illustrious Aldwinckle in London, using a process which is more than a hundred years old. These classic patterns are called *foulards,* and they are also used for the most sought-after English neckties.

The shirt in our photograph comes in a wide range of different colors—all in the impeccable tradition of English taste. The tailoring is on the loose side — very comfortable and informal. You can wear the shirt open or closed at the neck, and it is cut to be worn either inside your trousers or outside. The price is $10.95. At the most distinguished stores, or write C. F. Hathaway, Waterville, Maine.

TEN
YEARS:
TEN
LANDMARK
CAMPAIGNS

SCHWEPPES

Schweppes Although, like Hathaway, a campaign initiated in the fifties, the Schweppes Tonic invasion of the U.S. realized its full potential in the sixties. No collection of the best campaigns of that decade would be complete without its inclusion. Like so many of the others we have selected, the advertising for Schweppes added an extra value to the product itself. Commander Whitehead, both the chief executive and chief spokesman for Schweppes in the United States, was the personification of urbanity and sophistication. His use in the campaign, in retrospect a stroke of genius, was not so obvious at the beginning. Would a smooth, upper-class Brit appeal to a middle-class American audience? You bet he would. Particularly in the way he was presented by David Ogilvy.

To demonstrate in what great esteem a host held his guests, he served them Schweppes—and made sure that they were aware of the label. To treat yourself to this "special elixir," you purchased Schweppes even though it required the payment of a premium price. Millions paid it, happily. This special value did not result only from the product itself. It existed also as a result of the advertising.

The Man from Schweppes Arrives!

M EET Commander Edward Whitehead, Schweppesman Extraordinary from London, England, where the house of Schweppes has been famous since 1794.

The Commander recently arrived in these United States.

His mission? To make sure that every drop of Schweppes bottled in America has the *original flavor* which has made it the essential mixer for Tonic drinks all over the world.

Schweppes flavor, you will notice, is curiously refreshing. Schweppes has an almost astringent impact on the palate, with a delicious *bittersweet* aftertaste.

Today, the original Schweppes elixir (that's what gives Schweppes its unique flavor) is being imported from England and bottled in America. And now that Schweppes have given up the extravagant practice of transporting heavy bottles across 3,000 miles of Atlantic Ocean, you can buy their incomparable Tonic, for little more than ordinary mixers, at stores everywhere.

It took Schweppes almost a hundred years to bring their Tonic to its present perfection. But it will take *you* only thirty seconds to pick up the phone and order Schweppes from your storekeeper.

• • •

RETAILERS: For prompt service, please call Pepsi-Cola Bottling Co. of Pittsfield, 158 Tyler St., Pittsfield, Mass. Dial: 4579.

Schweppes now available in handy 6-bottle cartons of 10-oz. bottles.

Piutes greet Big Chief Tonic Water from over the seas!

Above, demonstrating the virtues of the original and authentic Schweppes Tonic to a group of original and authentic Americans, you see Commander Edward Whitehead — heap big chief of the whole Schweppes setup in America.

The Commander first arrived on our shores eight years ago — and you can see the results of his work all around you.

Today, there's hardly a living, breathing American who doesn't know that Schweppes is the only mixer for a *real* Gin-and-Tonic. Who hasn't tasted Schweppervescence — exuberant little bubbles that last your whole drink through.

Thanks to Commander Whitehead, Schweppes Tonic is now sold in 50 states of the Union.

So whether you mix yours with gin, or vodka, or rum — or drink it straight, like our friends in the picture — make sure you get the *real stuff*.

The one and only *Schweppes* Tonic. It's curiously refreshing.

TEN
YEARS:
TEN
LANDMARK
CAMPAIGNS

SCHWEPPES

MAN: Okay Joe. Fire away.

That's it. That's it. Hold it.

WHITEHEAD (OVER): Now for a
Schweppes Bitter Lemon.

Bottle upside down to see the
lemon morsels.

Schweppes has them because
Schweppes is made from whole
fresh lemons.

Schweppes Bitter Lemon is a
versatile mixer and an adult soft
drink. The only one children
don't like.

Thank goodness we invented it.
MUSIC: Rule Britannia.

FIRST MAN: Missed you,
Whitehead. Been away?

WHITEHEAD: Not really.
Hong Kong. Singapore.
Rangoon.

Good to be back, Mr. Garp. Missed
my Schweppes.
VOICE: Shhh!

FIRST MAN: Good stuff, Schweppes.
Curiously refreshing.

WHITEHEAD: Right. Jolly little
bubbles. Lasts the whole drink
through.
VOICE: Shhh!

FIRST MAN: Schweppervescence?

WHITEHEAD: Right.
Schweppervescence.

You know Schweppes is the only
mixer for authentic drinks.

What blazes, sir! Would you kindly
stop shushing me?

SECOND MAN: I'm not shushing
you at all, Commander. I was merely
trying to order another Schweppes.
Schweppes.

FIRST MAN/WHITEHEAD: Oh.

TEN
YEARS:
TEN
LANDMARK
CAMPAIGNS

SCHWEPPES

WHITEHEAD: Now wait. Don't tell me. Was it Hong Kong? Beirut? Cairo perhaps?

WOMAN: Guess again, Commander Whitehead.

WHITEHEAD: London. It was London.

WOMAN: I'll give you a hint. You were having a tonic and you were warning the waiter to make jolly well sure he mixed it with Schweppes.

WHITEHEAD: But that might have been anywhere. Schweppes' quinine water is famous all over the world.

WOMAN: In those days you used to say it was impossible to mix tonic without Schweppes.

WHITEHEAD: It is. No other mixer has Schweppes' bitter-sweet flavor and rare effervescence.

WOMAN: Effervescence? You used to call those little bubbles Schweppervescence.

WHITEHEAD: Schweppervescence. Of course. Those remarkable little bubbles that last the whole drink through.

Did you know that Schweppes quinine water is now bottled here in the states from the imported elixir?

Ah, but do tell me, where did we meet? Was it Paris?

Volvo *A layout pad, a typewriter and the talent to put them both to good use—you didn't need much more than that to land an important piece of new business in the comparatively simple sixties. "Full service" didn't carry too much weight with advertisers—what they cared about was creativity. To start the new agency they had in mind, Carl Ally, Amil Gargano and Jim Durfee needed a client—so they made a deal with Volvo. If they could create some ads that Volvo liked, the car's American distributor agreed to switch his account. For a few weeks, according to Durfee, every night after working at their regular jobs the three of them would meet at a gatehouse in Connecticut, where they created the ads that won the account. Just like that! Volvo made another successful change a few years later when, after a falling-out with Carl Ally, they turned the advertising over to a young copywriter who had done some of their ads at Ally. That's how Ed McCabe picked up the business—a nice shot in the arm for the brand-new partnership of Scali, McCabe, Sloves.*

It'll last longer than the payment book.

It takes about three years to go through a payment book.
It takes about eleven years to go through a Volvo.
That eleven years, incidentally, is based on the average life of a Volvo in Sweden, where there are no speed limits on the highways, where there are over 70,000 miles of unpaved roads, where driving is virtually a national pastime.
You may not want to keep your Volvo eleven years, but if you do, nobody will be the wiser. We don't follow the wasteful practice of making new models look different just to make old models look obsolete.
But no matter how long you keep your Volvo, you won't tire of it. A Volvo will run away from every other compact in its class, yet deliver over 25 miles to the gallon, even with automatic transmission.
Drive a Volvo at a nearby dealer. And don't look at it merely as a superb automobile.
Look at it more as a way to get out from under car payments into swimming pool, boat, or vacation house payments. After all, there's more to life than own- ing the newest car on the block. Even for us.

129

TEN
YEARS:
TEN
LANDMARK
CAMPAIGNS

VOLVO

Drive it like you hate it.

When Volvo came to the U.S. from Sweden in 1956, Chevy was the "hot one," Ford was the "safe one" and Volkswagen was just catching on as the "funny one."

We'd like to say that Volvo immediately caught on as the "tough one." It didn't.

At first only the "car nuts" bought it. They figured that if a Volvo could hold up under Swedish driving (no speed limits), survive Swedish roads (80% unpaved), withstand Swedish winters (30° below), that a Volvo would hold up under anything.

They figured right. Volvos were driven right off showroom floors onto race tracks where they proceeded to win more races than any other compact ever made.

Volvos are still winning races. But that isn't why they're bought today. Volvos are now being used and misused as family cars. They're safe. And on the highway they run away from other popular-priced compacts in every speed range, yet get over 25 miles to the gallon like the little economy cars.

Volvo is now called the "tough one." And it's the biggest-selling imported compact in America today.

You can drive a Volvo like you hate it for as little as $2565. * Cheaper than psychiatry.

*Manufacturer's suggested retail price East Coast Port of Entry. Overseas delivery available. See the Yellow Pages for the Volvo dealer nearest you.

How often do you buy a new car?
That's too often.

Buy a Volvo, keep it a long time and get out from under car payments for a change.

How long can you expect a Volvo to last? We're not sure yet how long a Volvo will hold up here in the States. In Sweden, Volvos are driven an average of eleven years. When you consider that there are no speed limits on the Swedish highways, there are over 70,000 miles of unpaved roads, and that driving is almost the national pastime in Sweden, you can understand why we have to bite our tongues to keep from making some rash promises.

One more thing. You won't *mind* keeping your Volvo a long time. Its body style doesn't change every year. It's uncomplicated and requires very little maintenance. It runs away from other popular-priced compacts in every speed range, yet gets over 25 miles to the gallon like the little economy cars (even with automatic transmission).

And your Volvo will look good standing next to your swimming pool. The one you build with the money that used to go for car payments.

See the Yellow Pages for the dealer nearest you.

TEN
YEARS:
TEN
LANDMARK
CAMPAIGNS

VOLVO

Would you sell your present car to a friend?

Why not? Because it's three or four years old and you figure you've gotten the best years out of it and who knows what's about to go wrong with it?

Volvo owners sell to friends. And they don't lose their friends.

In fact, so many Volvos pass from friend to friend that Volvos are hard to find on used car lots. And when you do find one you pay a good price for it.

The reason Volvos hold up so well is that Volvos are built in Sweden. In Sweden it's tough being a car. In Sweden Volvos are driven hard. Yet they're driven an average of eleven years before people give up on them.

In America it looks like Volvos will do as well. We don't guarantee how long they'll last, but we do know people don't give up on them here, either. Of all the Volvos registered here during the last eleven years, 95% of them are still on the road.

You may not want to keep your Volvo eleven years (although once you get used to *not* making car payments you might). But wouldn't it be a comfort to own a car that's built well enough to be driven that long?

Especially since you can always sell it to a friend at a good price. With a clear conscience. ©Volvo, Inc.

See the Yellow Pages for the dealer nearest you. He can also arrange delivery overseas.

A lifetime supply of Volvos.

According to statistics, the average American drives 50 years in his lifetime.

The average car is traded in on a new one every three years and three months.

Which means if you drive an average number of years, in average cars, you'll own 15.1 cars in your lifetime.

Fortunately, there is a way to beat the averages. You do it by owning only above-average cars: Volvos. Volvos are built so well and last so long that just 4.5 of them could solve your driving problems for life.

This is based on your keeping each Volvo 11 years. Which is not only possible, but probable.

It's possible because Volvos last an average of 11 years in Sweden where it's tough being a car.

We don't *guarantee* they'll last that long here, where being a car is relatively easy. But we do know that over 95% of all the Volvos registered here in the last 11 years are still on the road.

It's probable because there is a strong argument for hanging on to a Volvo once you get your hands on one. It's called money.

If you buy 4.5 Volvos in your lifetime instead of 15.1 average cars, you save on the price of 10.6 cars. At $3,260 per car (the average price paid for a new car these days, according to the Automobile Manufacturers Association) you get $34,556. Add to this approximately $5,000 in interest on car loans that you don't have to pay and you get a whopping $39,556.

Which is enough to buy a half-dozen college educations or a whole house.

From a straight dollars and cents point of view there is much to be said for owning only Volvos. And that's really the only point of view worth considering.

TEN
YEARS:
TEN
LANDMARK
CAMPAIGNS

VOLVO

The execution is different, but the concept is basically the same.

Both vehicles are very difficult to destroy.

However, the M-41 (at right) was built to withstand slightly meaner treatment than the Volvo 144 (at left).

As a result, the M-41 weighs in at 50,000 lbs. And for all its bulk, carries only four men—in extreme discomfort, we might add.

It gets 1.4 miles to the gallon and won't go over 40 miles an hour.

In other words, it's a tank.

The Volvo, on the other hand, weighs in at just 2,600 lbs. And for all its lack of bulk, carries five men—in extreme comfort.

It gets substantially better gas mileage and will go fast enough to attract police cars. Which are faster but not as strong.

In other words, a Volvo is strong in the way a tank is strong and has strengths where a tank has weaknesses.

Just how strong is a Volvo?

You could stack eight Volvos, one on top of another, without disturbing the Volvo on the bottom. That's a total of 10 tons. Six steel pillars, boxed for maximum strength, support the roof. (It's ironic that Detroit calls cars with no steel pillars "hardtops," when in reality they're just the opposite.)

Each side of the Volvo body is made from one solid piece of steel. There are no weak points because there are no seams. In other parts of the body, where seams occur, 8,000 spot welds fuse them together.

It's this kind of construction that once led Car & Driver Magazine to make the following observation.

"...the Volvo is possibly the toughest vehicle anywhere this side of the Aberdeen Proving Grounds and there is a growing legion of happy owners who will be glad to verify the point."

The Aberdeen Proving Grounds, incidentally, is where the U. S. Army tests tanks.

It even has armor-plating.

Volvo has a finish six coats thick. First the body is etched in zinc phosphate so the paint gets a vise-like grip on the metal. Then it's dunked in rustproofing primer. The body then gets one undercoat, one sealer coat and three color coats of baked enamel. 33 lbs. of protection in all.

It's because of this that you hear stories like this . . .

One day a friend of this writer told of an experience with a dent in the door of his Volvo. He had it repaired and noticed that the shop charged him a modest sum for body work but nothing for paint. Being honest, he raised the point. The body man explained that after banging out the dent, the paint was still undamaged—so there was no need for a re-paint!

A Volvo doesn't self-destruct in three years.

There is an obvious advantage in owning a car that's built like a Volvo. Once it's paid for, there's still something left to own.

A Volvo can help you fight off the impulse that drives you into debt every few years. Because by keeping it, you can begin making payments to yourself instead of the finance company.

Of course, if you're not interested in adding money to your coffers, you can sell your Volvo after three years. And delight in how little you lose.

Volvos depreciate as slowly as they disintegrate.

Is this 36-page paperback the story of your life?

The average new car is bought with the understanding that it will be paid off within 36 months.

Unfortunately, the average new car is unloaded by its owner after 32 months.

The result is, you're buried under car payments for as long as you drive an average car.

The only way to beat this ingenious plan, short of becoming a pedestrian, is to buy a car that'll outlast a payment book.

A Volvo is built to outlast two, three, maybe even four payment books. 9 out of every 10 Volvos registered here in the last eleven years are still on the road.

And while we can't guarantee that your Volvo will survive eleven years, it should definitely last long enough to obscure the memory of monthly payments.

Our claims are exceeded only by the claims of impartial car experts, who sometimes go even farther than we would dare.

According to Road Test Magazine: "Buying a Volvo is like getting married; you only expect to have to do it once."

135

TEN
YEARS:
TEN
LANDMARK
CAMPAIGNS

**BENSON
& HEDGES
100's**

Benson & Hedges 100's *In 1967, Wells, Rich, Greene took what could have been a product gimmick—an extra-long cigarette—an idea that could have been a fad, transitory, insignificant, and turned it into a hot and growing product category. And they did it by presenting, with unfailing good humor and wit, the many disadvantages of smoking extra-long Benson & Hedges cigarettes.*

Once again a cardinal rule of advertising—

according to the researchers and rules writers—had been broken. As if such a "rule" ever really existed. Wells, Rich, Greene sold positively—negatively. If the Surgeon General and the FCC had not forced cigarette advertising off the air the Benson & Hedges campaign would probably still have us laughing and buying and puffing. Much of the credit for the effectiveness of the Benson & Hedges campaign should also go to a former still photographer, Howard Zieff, who was the

cinematographer on all of Benson & Hedges' classic commercials. Zieff was undoubtedly the most celebrated and successful TV commercial photographer and director of the sixties. Using Benson & Hedges and other campaigns as a springboard, he went to Hollywood in the early seventies—fashioning a new career as a feature film director.

MUSIC: Benson & Hedges Theme throughout.
HEDGES: Good evening. My name is Byron Hedges and I know a lot of you've been asking how me and Mr. Benson got together.

I first sampled Benson's rich tobacco blend by pure chance and I knew I had to find him.

MAN: He keeps calling for someone named Benson.

HEDGES: But then on the brink of despair....

BENSON: Hey get your Benson's. Get your nice Bens...

...You know where I can find that man?

...MAN: Benson?

...HEDGES: Yeah.

...MAN: Never heard of him.

HEDGES: My search continued. BENSON!   BENSON!

...HEDGES: You know the man who makes
...hese?

BENSON: You're looking at 'im.

HEDGES: Yes. Benson had the great tobacco,
and I had the biggest idea since king-size.
I can see it now. Hedges & Benson 100's.
Of course Benson saw it a little different.

TEN
YEARS:
TEN
LANDMARK
CAMPAIGNS

**BENSON
& HEDGES
100's**

MUSIC: Benson & Hedges Theme
throughout.

VOICE OVER: If we had made the longer
Benson & Hedges 100's a long time ago
we might never have known the British
were coming.

The law of gravity might have gone
completely unnoticed for a long, long time.

The discovery of electricity might have
been fifty years later.

For the love of five extra puffs the Delaware
might never have been crossed.

Can you imagine what would
have happened if Adam smoked?

TEN
YEARS:
TEN
LANDMARK
CAMPAIGNS

**BENSON
& HEDGES
100's**

MUSIC: Benson & Hedges Theme
throughout.

TEN
YEARS:
TEN
LANDMARK
CAMPAIGNS

**BENSON
& HEDGES
100's**

MUSIC: Benson & Hedges Theme throughout.

FIRST MAN: French onion soup.
Roast Long Island duck.
SECOND MAN: Um.

FIRST MAN: Cherries Jubilee.

VOICE OVER: When you're down to your last
Benson & Hedges 100

ECOND MAN: Um.

FIRST MAN: Hot cup of coffee.
SECOND MAN: Ummm.

FIRST MAN/SECOND MAN: A cigarette.

s nice to know that just one puff is
rich, so full of flavor,

that one Benson & Hedges can last
you a long,

long time if it has to.

TEN
YEARS:
TEN
LANDMARK
CAMPAIGNS

TALON

Talon *Our final vote goes to the print campaign for Talon zippers, created by Delehanty, Kurnit & Geller, an agency that has subsequently undergone numerous changes of name and ownership. Like many other campaigns in our select group, it was produced for a relatively small advertiser using very little money, even by the standards of the day. The impact of the campaign, funny and single-minded as it was, was felt at many levels. Consumers actually sought out and expressed a preference for garments that used Talon zippers, as opposed to no-name fasteners. Apparel manufacturers, in order to sell their clothing more rapidly, cooperated willingly with Talon by displaying Talon I.D. tags on their merchandise. This modest but highly effective campaign played a major role for a long time in keeping Talon prosperous. Talon became a household word—synonymous with quality—thanks to advertising.*

A number of young and unknown copywriters and art directors who were destined to become some of the biggest names in the business—among them Jerry Della Femina, Ron Travisano and Peter Hirsch—worked on this comparatively small account for a comparatively small but "hot" agency. It paid off for everybody involved. And once again, doubters to the contrary, humor had proved itself to be an inspired way to achieve a desired sales result.

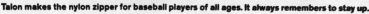

Delehanty Kurnit & Geller copywriter Jerry Della Femina and art director Ron Travisano had a terrific idea—why not create a comic strip ad (always high readership scores!) and get the whole Peanuts gang to pitch for Talon? It didn't work out that way, because <u>Peanuts</u> creator Charles Schulz wouldn't play ball with them. When creative director Peter Hirsch recalled that many Italian comic strips effectively used photographs instead of cartoons, he suggested they take another swing at it. This ad was the result. A home run!

She's got her father's eyes and her mother's zipper.

Lucky girl.

She has diaper service, instant formula, a wardrobe of stretch-wear. And now, Talon Zephyr® nylon zipper...the ultimate fashion closure.

It's the slimmest, gentlest, most flexible zipper in the world.

You will make sure to get all your infant's and children's stretch-wear with Talon Zephyrs, won't you?

After all, doesn't the softest zipper ever made belong next to the softest little people?

ZEPHYR A REG. TRADEMARK OF TALON, INC. © 1964 BY TALON, INC. MEADVILLE, PA./MEXICO, TALON de MEXICO S.A. de C.V./CANADA, LIGHTNING FASTENER CO., LTD.

10

TEN
YEARS:
TEN
LANDMARK
CAMPAIGNS

TALON

LAST NIGHT MRS. MARY POWERS OPENED ON BROADWAY.

It definitely wasn't the break she had been waiting for. But her popped zipper was the most unforgettable event of the season for everyone else.

And to think it all could have been avoided if she had been zipped up with one of our Talon Zephyr nylon zippers.

The Talon Zephyr won't snag, grab, bind, slip, snap, crackle, or pop.

On, or off, Broadway.

A prominent New York stockbroker just went public.

It's bad enough when the market takes a sudden plunge.

But when your trouser zipper goes down, you lose another kind of security.

So for your own good, look for the Talon Zephyr®nylon zipper next time you buy yourself a suit or a pair of slacks.

The Zephyr zipper is designed not to snag, or jam. And a little device called Memory Lock® will make sure your zipper stays up.

So all you'll have to worry about going down are your stocks.

TEN
YEARS:
TEN
LANDMARK
CAMPAIGNS

TALON

Try to act nonchalant.
After all, it happens to the best of us.
Or at least, it used to. Until Talon invented Memory-Lock®, the ingenious, self-locking device that makes it impossible—repeat: impossible—for the Talon 42 trouser zipper to slip open accidentally. Even if you forget to press down the pull-tab.
Add *that* to your list of great achievements of Western Man.

TALON, INC., MEADVILLE, PA./MEXICO: TALON de MEXICO S.A. de CV./CANADA: LIGHTNING FASTENER CO., LTD./© 1963 BY TALON, INC.

"My fly used to open 50 times a day."

By Bob Veder

Every day the guys at work would take bets on how many ups and downs I'd have before lunch.

Till I finally bought a pair of pants with this special Talon 42 zipper in the fly. See, the Talon zipper has this built-in gizmo called Memory Lock, that won't let a guy's zipper do anything he don't want it to.

Like slide and slip all over the place when he's sliding and slipping all over the place.

Man, I never knew how easy it was holding a pavement-pounder till I was able to use both hands.

TEN
YEARS:
TEN
LANDMARK
CAMPAIGNS

TALON

Too bad. It was your big chance.
Playing a spoon solo on the Amateur Hour.

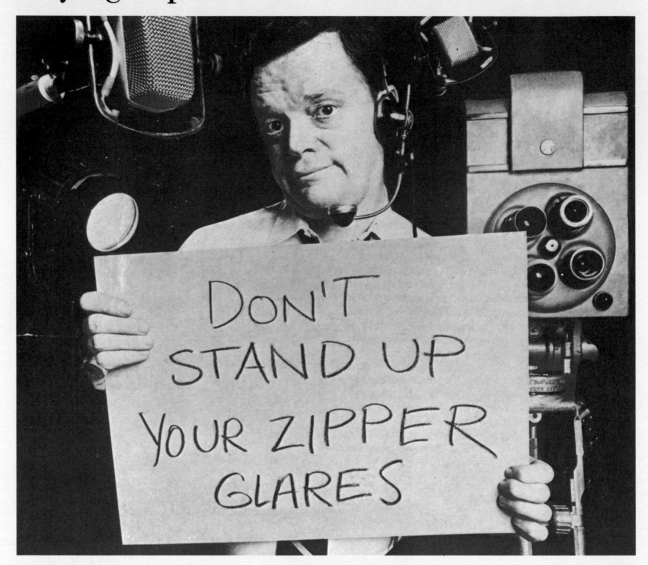

Isn't it ridiculous to let a zipper stand in the way of success. But those shiny metal ones with the big gleaming teeth will do it every time. And why! When it's so easy to avoid. With the Talon Zephyr* nylon trouser zipper. The one that doesn't glitter in a spotlight. Or the sun. Or anywhere.

So the next time that big chance comes along, don't muff it. Let your performance shine, not your zipper. Make sure you're wearing trousers with Talon Zephyr*, the nylon zipper. And give our regards to Broadway.

TEN YEARS:
TEN
LANDMARK
ADS

6 Perhaps the most remarkable thing about the great print advertising of the sixties is how completely it broke with the past. It looked and sounded nothing at all like any advertising that had ever preceded it.

The forties had segued into the fifties. Advertising during that twenty year span had not been all that different. Illustrations, type faces, designs and copy appeals couldn't clearly be labeled "forties" or "fifties." They were pretty much interchangeable. Even the type-heavy narrative advertising of the thirties provided a clue as to what advertising would say and look like in the years to come. It was easy to see how advertising had evolved.

Until the sixties.

Nothing had quite prepared us for the creative revolution. Art and copy worked together, one completing the thought or making the point for the other. It was a unifying, synergistic creativity that produced the most effective and exciting advertising ever seen. Photography replaced graphics. The product became larger than life—backgrounds were clean and clutter eliminated. Reality was in. Hyperbole was out. To understand how startling this was, consider that print advertising of the sixties looks like today, sounds like today, and with appropriate but modest adjustments, could work today. Advertising of the fifties, on the other hand, would appear hopelessly out-of-date.

The creative revolution elevated standards throughout the industry. Hundreds upon hundreds of superb ads were created. It was enormously difficult for us to choose just ten. For print advertising particularly, the golden age of the sixties was pure 24 karat. We don't believe any of our selections show their age.

Wolfschmidt Vodka *If Sam Bronfman of the House of Seagram knew his whisky, he also knew talent. With Chivas Regal safely in the hands of DDB he turned over his new vodka entry, Wolfschmidt, to Papert, Koenig, Lois, the first of the new creative shops to be formed in the sixties. Their mission: to do battle with mighty Smirnoff.*

If there ever was a liquor category in which advertising could make a difference, it had to be vodka. After all, what product other than vodka would have a sales leader that advertised it had no taste and left you breathless? If a beverage had no taste, what distinguished it from its competitors? The creative combination of George Lois and Julian Koenig didn't take too long to zero in on that potential opportunity.

The Wolfschmidt ad shown here had an immediate and positive effect. It had the clean, lean design that was a Lois trademark, and the effortless copy of Julian Koenig. Wolfschmidt's superb advertising called attention to itself, but it also performed wonders for the brand. Wolfschmidt was instantly established as the second premium vodka. Although Smirnoff's leadership was never seriously threatened, PKL instantly and credibly positioned Wolfschmidt as a viable and prestigious option.

The interesting (phallic?) way in which the bottle was shown in the ad, the slick graphics that look as fresh today as they did in the early sixties, the calculated use of white space, the perfect marriage of copy and art, all provide a capsule case history of how fast and how far the creative revolution had come.

Wolfschmidt sales climbed, and so did the recognition of PKL as a hot, creative shop. As Wolfschmidt might prove to be an acceptable alternative to Smirnoff, so might PKL be an acceptable alternative to DDB. Papert, Koenig, Lois was an agency to watch.

"You're some tomato.
We could make beautiful Bloody Marys together.
I'm different from those other fellows."

"I like you, Wolfschmidt.
You've got taste."

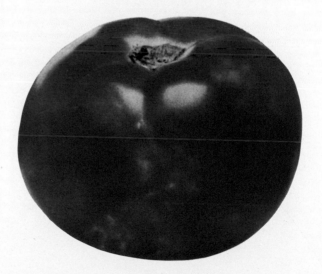

Wolfschmidt Vodka has the touch of taste that marks genuine old world vodka. Wolfschmidt in a Bloody Mary is a tomato in triumph. Wolfschmidt brings out the best in every drink. General Wine and Spirits Company, N.Y. 22. Made from Grain, 80 or 100 Proof. Prod. of U.S.A.

It's easy, when you know how.

Once we merely breathed the air, now [we] inhabit it.

Millions of people have flown. And the [lar]gest percentage did it on American [Air]lines.

American's know-how is one reason [fly]ing is easy today. We've made so [m]any contributions to flying, that our [hi]story reads like a history of com[m]ercial aviation itself.

For instance, the DC-3, the plane that <u>made</u> commercial aviation, was built to American's specifications.

The first non-stop, round-trip, transcontinental service was on an American DC-7, also built to our specifications.

We were the airline to pioneer weather radar. The first to have transcontinental jet service. The first to build a jet-age maintenance plant. The first airline to be equipped with DME (Distance Measuring Equipment), the most significant advance ever made in airline navigation, even beyond radar.

Today, American offers 707 Astrojets,* the first commercial planes powered with fan-jets, the engines that opened Jet Age: Stage II.

When experienced travellers pick an airline, it's usually American. And there are obvious reasons why.

AMERICAN AMERICA'S LEADING AIRLINE

American Airlines *An aviation ad without an airplane? Or a timetable? Or a stewardess? Or a pilot? Or a passenger enjoying a sumptuous repast? Unthinkable, except that Doyle Dane Bernbach had run just such ads a few years before on a much smaller scale for a much smaller airline, El Al, to a much smaller audience.*

Now, in the nation's largest magazines and most important newspapers, here was arguably America's number-one airline telling the world that it was "easy when you know how." And what was the illustration? An American eagle, naturally.

Horn & Hardart *It would be nice to think that, somehow, between the good food offered by Horn & Hardart and the good ads done by Carl Ally's agency, the automat could have withstood the onrush of both the fast-food joints and the chic new restaurants that catered to New York's upwardly mobile crowd. Unfortunately, Horn & Hardart did not succeed in either instance. Fast food and fancy food—they both beat up on the automat. In fact, Horn & Hardart's current management converted many of the old-fashioned automats into newfangled fast-food emporiums. If you can't lick 'em, join 'em. The automat didn't survive, but the ads were great.*

In the sixties, the automats were living on borrowed time, although they didn't know it yet. Business was still good, thanks to a brassy and sassy campaign conceived by copywriter Ed McCabe (also responsible, in part, for Volvo's tough-sounding copy) and art director Ron Barrett.

Like so many other ads selected for this collection, it is but one part of a great series. Any one of the automat ads could have been chosen. They are all equally memorable, equally convincing.

You can't eat atmosphere.

Horn & Hardart. It's not fancy. But it's good.

Rolls-Royce *According to David Ogilvy's own recollection, this Rolls-Royce ad, which is vividly recalled by so many advertising professionals more than twenty years after it first appeared, was published only once, in just two newspapers and two magazines. Its initial success and subsequent recall by readers represent an amazing accomplishment, considering that there was nothing exceptional about its traditional luxury car photograph and austere factual copy. But there was real power and imagery in the headline. This ad, written by Ogilvy himself, provides the most convincing support for Bill Bernbach's contention that the public responds to ideas, not to advertising techniques.*

/

The Rolls-Royce Silver Cloud II – $15,655 P.O.E. Delivery costs slightly higher in Alaska and Hawaii.

"At 60 miles an hour the loudest noise in this new Rolls-Royce comes from the electric clock"

What __makes__ Rolls-Royce the best car in the world? "There is really no magic about it—it is merely patient attention to detail," says an eminent Rolls-Royce engineer.

1. "At 60 miles an hour the loudest noise comes from the electric clock," reports the Technical Editor of THE MOTOR. The silence inside the car is uncanny. Three exhaust mufflers tune out sound frequencies—acoustically.

2. Every Rolls-Royce engine is run for four hours at full throttle before installation, and each car is extensively test-driven over varying road surfaces. Every Rolls-Royce has its "History Book"—an *eleven-page* signed record of all operations and inspections performed on the car. This goes into the Company's permanent files.

3. The Rolls-Royce Silver Cloud II is designed as an *owner-driven* car. It has power steering, power brakes and automatic gear-shift. It is very easy to drive and to park. Women handle the car with ease.

4. The finished car spends a week in the final test shop, being fine-tuned. Here it is subjected to ninety-eight separate ordeals. For example, the engineers use a stethoscope to listen for axle-whine. Silent operation of every part is the standard for acceptance.

5. The new eight-cylinder aluminium engine is even more powerful than the previous six-cylinder unit, *yet it weighs ten pounds less.* It accelerates from zero to 60 miles an hour in 11.4 seconds. (ROAD AND TRACK test report.)

6. The coachwork is given as many as *nine* coats of finishing paint—*hand rubbed.*

7. Every Rolls-Royce takes the "Monsoon Test." Windows are rolled up and the car is pelted with water and air at gale force. *Not a drop may come through.*

8. By moving a switch on the steering column, you can adjust the shock-absorbers to suit road conditions. (The lack of fatigue in driving this car is remarkable.)

9. Another switch defrosts the rear window, by heating a network of 1360 almost invisible wires in the glass.

10. The seats are upholstered with eight hides of English leather—enough to make 128 pairs of soft shoes.

11. A picnic table, fashioned of inlaid French walnut, slides out from under the dash. Two more swing out behind the front seats.

12. The engine cooling fan is *lopsided.* Its five blades are unequally spaced and pitched to take thick and thin slices of air. Thus it does its work in a *whisper.* The company goes to fantastic lengths to ensure peace and quiet for the occupants of the car.

13. There are *three* independent brake linkages. The Rolls-Royce is a very *safe* car—and also a very responsive and *lively* car. It cruises serenely at eighty-five. Top speed is in excess of 100 m.p.h.

14. The gas tank cannot be opened without the driver's consent: *you* unlock it electrically from a button on the dash.

15. Automatic transmission, power brakes and power steering are *standard.* So are the radio, heating and ventilating equipment, walnut panelling, seats adjustable for tilt and rake, and white sidewall tires. The Rolls-Royce people do not designate essential equipment as "optional extras."

16. The Bentley is made by Rolls-Royce. Except for the radiator shells, they are identical motor cars, manufactured by the same engineers in the same works.

The Bentley costs $300 less, because its radiator is simpler to make. People who feel diffident about driving a Rolls-Royce can buy a Bentley.

ROLLS-ROYCE AND BENTLEY

PRICE. The car shown above costs $15,655 P.O.E. Delivery costs slightly higher in Alaska and Hawaii.

If you would like to try driving a Rolls-Royce or Bentley, write or telephone any dealer listed below. For further information or complete list of U. S. dealers, write Mr. Richard L. Yorke, Vice President, Rolls-Royce Inc., Room 465, 45 Rockefeller Plaza, New York, N. Y.

159

Western Union *A scrawling red "X" runs through the copy of a famous Chivas Regal ad that bears the heading "Don't bother to read this ad, just taste Chivas Regal." Despite this negative suggestion, it's safe to assume that everybody who saw it made a point of reading every word. What does all this have to do with Western Union? The negative psychology expressed in the Western Union headline, "Ignore it," was identical to that of the Chivas ad, and equally successful. By showing an actual telegram, Benton & Bowles, the agency that created the ad, used the printed page for a product demonstration. This technique is frequently employed by successful advertisers and often results in very memorable advertising. Polaroid ads almost always used the page for a demonstration of instant photography's most important benefit—the pleasure and satisfaction one feels upon seeing a finished photograph within sixty seconds.*

Xerox ads were product demonstrations more often than not. Volvo advertising regularly demonstrated the product's principal attributes: strength and safety. The list goes on. The writer of the Western Union ad summed up the essence of all the reasons that have ever existed to send a telegram, and he did it in just two words. Further, those two words defied conventional advertising wisdom and the "rules" once again. They accentuated the negative, with positive results.

TEN
YEARS:
TEN
LANDMARK
ADS

160

Ignore it

WESTERN UNION
TELEGRAM

CLASS OF SERVICE

This is a fast message unless its deferred character is indicated by the proper symbol.

W. P. MARSHALL, PRESIDENT

1201 (4-60)

SYMBOLS

DL = Day Letter
NL = Night Letter
LT = International Letter Telegram

The filing time shown in the date line on domestic telegrams is LOCAL TIME at point of origin. Time of receipt is LOCAL TIME at point of destination

IGNORE A TELEGRAM? YOU CAN'T. NO ONE EVER IGNORED
A TELEGRAM. YOUR TELEGRAM ALWAYS COMPELS IMMEDIATE
ATTENTION -- AND IMMEDIATE RESPONSE.

TO BE SURE TO GET ACTION, SEND A TELEGRAM.

THE COMPANY WILL APPRECIATE SUGGESTIONS FROM ITS PATRONS CONCERNING ITS SERVICE

Polaroid *Here's another advertising triumph that could very well have been included in our top ten campaigns, because DDB's campaign for Polaroid has all the hallmarks of greatness. It's not only memorable, but it also helped create a completely new product category. Advertising never once permitted consumers to regard the Polaroid invention as a gimmick, fad or an extension of existing photography. Instead, it helped win acceptance for Dr. Land's remarkable invention as a whole system of photography made possible by Polaroid's totally new technology.*

Consequently, any one of dozens upon dozens of equally outstanding Polaroid ads could have been selected for this collection. We particularly like the one pictured here because it combines the power of a demonstration, the sense of participation and a substantial dose of wit and humor. Many Polaroid ads were touching or filled with wholesome humor, yet they all had a deadly serious purpose: to win converts to Polaroid from giant Kodak. During the sixties, millions upon millions of people discovered and delighted in Polaroid photography, because it was difficult not to feel and share in the excitement and surprise of Polaroid advertising—which brought readers right into the picture.

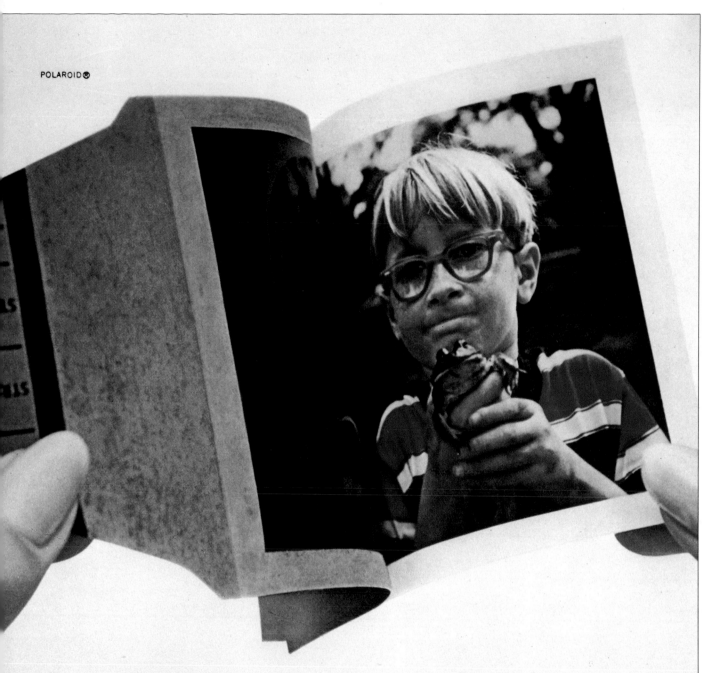

It's like opening a present.

Shown: Model 100, under $150, including flash.

Polaroid
Color Pack
Cameras
start at
under $60.

Eagle Shirts *Despite the fact that it's been twenty or more years since we last saw an Eagle shirt ad in* The New Yorker *magazine, we smiled at the recollection of an advertising man with the audacity to run a single advertisement in two parts in two separate issues of a magazine. That's what the late Howard Gossage did for another of his clients, Irish Whiskies. In fact, ad number one came to an abrupt end in the middle of a sentence. Gossage was both zany and brilliant. His advertising attracted fans who anticipated the appearance of his work in* The New Yorker *in much the same manner that devotees of the daily TV soaps await the next episode. Gossage probably could have written about any subject he chose with equal facility. Although he was wildly creative, his copy was on target and he always hit what he aimed at. Measured results proved that.*

One of his famous Eagle shirt promotions featured a color-naming contest. Try these winners on for size: See Red, Favor Curry, Holler Copper, Free Loden, Robert Shaw Coral, Lawsy Miss Scarlett and 'Enry 'Iggins Just You White. Crazy? Like a fox. Nobody had ever heard of Eagle shirts before this modest campaign began. Chances are, everyone exposed to Howard Gossage's ads will probably never forget Eagle shirts.

For this collection, we've chosen a two-page Eagle ad that's unusual even by Gossage's unconventional standards. It featured a front and back page and a special hybrid gift that was offered to readers.

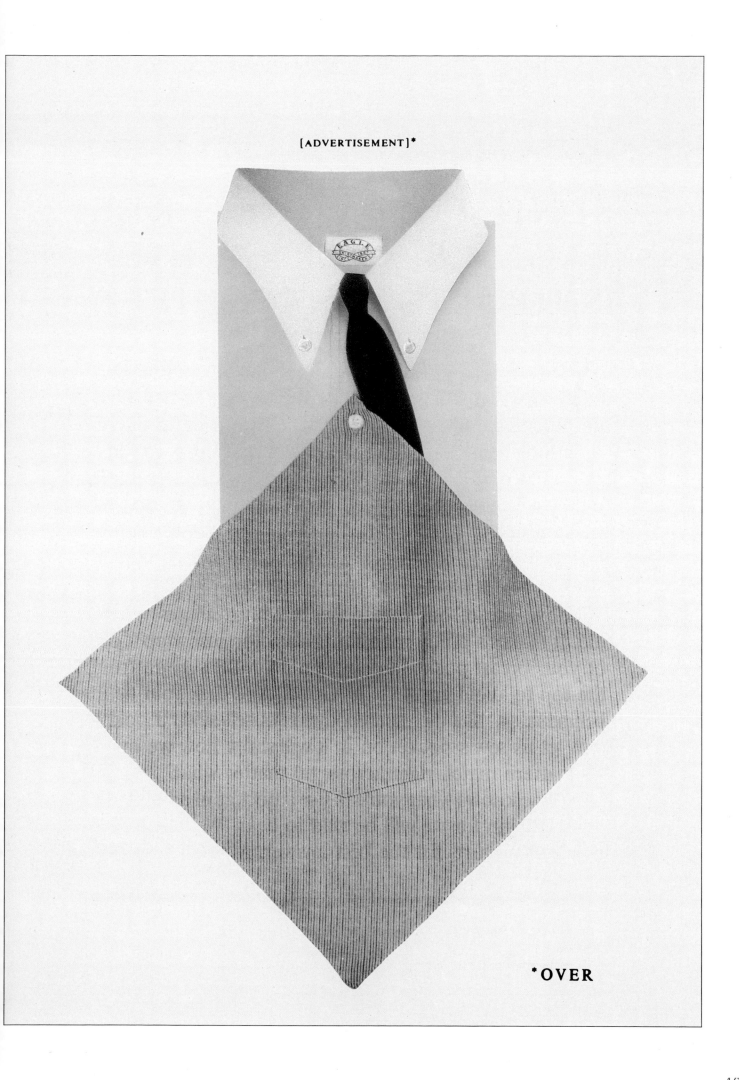

*OVER

165

[cont. from preceding page]

SEND FOR YOUR FREE EAGLE SHIRTKERCHIEF (SHIRTKIN?) (NAPCHIEF?)

AS far as we know this is a brand new invention. Perhaps you will be able to figure out how to realize its full potential. ★ It all started when we tried to devise something to send you—short of an actual shirt—to illustrate a few of the fine points of fine shirt making. A sample to take with you when you go shirt shopping. ★ So first we hemmed a piece of fine shirting; *20 stitches to the inch*, just like in our shirts. At this point you could still call it a handkerchief. ★ But it did seem a shame not to show one of our threadchecked buttonholes, so we did. It makes a pretty good shirt protector: just whip it out of your breast pocket and button it on the second from the top to avoid gravy spots. Good. And tuck your tie in behind it. ★ But then somebody in Pockets said, "Look, if you let us sew a pocket on it, it will show how we make the pattern match right across, no matter what." ★ So if anyone knows what you can use a pocket in a handkerchief/napkin for we will be glad to hear. We will give a half-dozen shirts for the best answer. Make it a dozen.

Eagle Shirtmakers, Quakertown, Pa.
Gentlemen :
Please send me whatever it is. (Signed)_____

Address_____City_____State_____

Gossage was not only confident that his brand of humor worked, he put it to the test in almost every ad he created. Long before "direct response" became a fashionable advertising technique, Gossage made coupons and write-ins an integral part of his creative strategy. He expected results. And he got them. For his clients and for himself.

How many Afflerbach Fellowships, Eagle labels and "shirtkerchiefs" were distributed? Who knows? Like his ads, Howard Gossage remains alive and well—but only in memory.

Dansk Designs *This small company in Mt. Kisco, New York, markets wonderfully crafted, wonderfully useful utensils and accessories: bowls, dishes, candlestick holders, flatware and more. Each item has the appearance of fine sculpture. How does an advertiser like this get the message out? With unfailing taste—so that the appearance of the advertising tells you something about the company's concern for quality and style.*

From the very beginning of the sixties and before, Dansk designs were interpreted in advertising by some of the most important talents of the creative revolution. Management insisted upon the best and invested heavily in exquisite graphics, photography and copy—despite a budget much too small to interest most advertising agencies. Probably no advertiser of the sixties, of any size, employed more celebrated and honored photographers than Dansk. The roster reads like a "Who's Who" of that era: Bert Stern, Carl Fischer, Onofrio Paccione, Irving Penn, and Mike Cuesta—and this list is probably not complete.

Dansk began the sixties with its advertising in the extremely competent hands of the boutique-sized Irving Serwer agency. But by 1962, this responsibility was turned over to the exciting new team of Papert, Koenig, Lois. Quality, craftsmanship and creativity continued at a high level.

Nevertheless, it wasn't long before Dansk management requested that Lou Dorfsman, the award-winning CBS art director and designer, take over from PKL. Naturally, standards continued high. In 1966 this timeless and elegant Dansk ad was designed by Dorfsman. The lovely and delicate photograph was the work of Mike Cuesta, while Judy Blumenthal, an award-winning Leber Katz Paccione copywriter, free-lanced the assignment, as she did many others for Dansk.

This ad, the only one in this collection not created within the formal agency structure, proves again that good work doesn't care where it comes from.

Consider the egg. Dansk did. One of nature's most satisfying and useful forms, it signifies the beginning of things. The beginning of Dansk things was 10 years ago, when this first Fjord spoon was hand-forged. Its success egged us on to create a number of other fine objects. Tawny teakwood bowls. A candlestick crowned with twelve thin tapers. Dusky Flamestone cups. An enamelled casserole as bright as a sunflower. And linens with rainbows in their warp and woof. Today there are 493 Dansk designs. Every one made for daily use. And not an everyday piece in the lot. They all appear in a new 96-page book, a book with the good form to be absolutely free. Write Dansk Designs Ltd, Dept. O, Mount Kisco, N.Y.

Cheese of Holland *A most unlikely participant in the creative revolution was an advertising agency with an image as cumbersome as its name: Erwin Wasey, Ruthrauff & Ryan. The result of a pre-sixties merger, this staid old shop was recognized more for its business acumen than its creative abilities.*

From time to time the agency attracted and employed top talent. It also provided a pleasant and supportive work environment, so the creative teams stayed around for a while, hoping that management would relate to advertising's new look and develop the enthusiasm to sell it. That never really happened. So, sooner or later, most of the good people departed. Unfortunately, Erwin Wasey, Ruthrauff & Ryan never altered the commonly held perception of an agency stumbling to catch up to the sixties.

All the more surprising and pleasing, therefore, is the fact that this beautifully written and designed ad came from EW, R & R. The agency had handled the account for a good many years, and the creative work was consistently well above average. In fact, in the late fifties, art director Ralph Ammirati had been responsible for designing some striking ads for this advertiser.

But it was in 1962 that the agency's effort really peaked. This memorable ad was created by a couple of those good people that arrived at Erwin Wasey, Ruthrauff & Ryan, liked the place, settled in for a few years and turned out lovely work like this. Design was by art director Sam Ferraro, copy by Ed Molyneaux, and Mike Cuesta added another notch to his knockout belt with this striking photo. "Life is short." This ad is great.

Pâté costs more than liverwurst.
Bisque costs more than soup.
Stroganoff costs more than stew.
This cheese costs more than other Edam.

Life is short.

CHEESE OF HOLLAND

Clairol *One of the most notable copy lines in the history of the business was written in the late fifties by a woman from Brooklyn, Shirley Polykoff. But as with the Hathaway campaign, the maturing and flowering of the creative effort—and the payoff—occurred in the sixties. The line? "Does she ... or doesn't she?" Five words that led to controversy, a change in American mores, a long-running campaign and substantial rewards for the advertiser, the agency and Ms. Polykoff. The response to the question was found immediately in the subhead that followed: "Hair color so natural only her hairdresser knows for sure."*

It's more a sorry commentary on where we were than a cause for celebration regarding how far we've come when we recall that Ms. Polykoff's copy was questioned and her ad was withheld from publication by self-appointed male censors. They believed that the double entendre "Does she ... or doesn't she?" was much too suggestive—despite the explanation in the subhead that made everything perfectly clear. Today it seems almost quaint.

But that wasn't the case years ago. To imply that Shirley Polykoff had something other than hair color on her mind when she wrote the line, as some did, was both insulting and an attempt at mind reading. To the credit of Clairol and its agency, Foote, Cone & Belding, they battled to save the campaign, successfully.

Shirley Polykoff needed no more support for her point of view than that given by the women who saw the ad. They knew exactly what it was talking about. Hair coloring—not hanky-panky—was on their minds. Clairol's sales skyrocketed. The idea of using hair color to achieve a more youthful look grew beyond the exotic Hollywood environment to which it had been almost exclusively confined and entered mainstream culture all over the U.S.

Although Polykoff's emotional and involving copy demonstrated a clear understanding of the way American attitudes had begun to change in the early sixties, the look of this landmark ad lagged years behind. Foote, Cone & Belding, a respected but very traditional agency, had not yet adopted the creative team concept. This was strictly a copywriter's ad. The fifties-style layout was almost incidental, undistinguished and contributed little toward furthering the idea. Copy alone carried this ad to the heights of recognition and effectiveness that it achieved.

"Does she ... or doesn't she?" became the stuff of legend, and carried Shirley Polykoff right into the Advertising Copywriters' Hall of Fame.

Does she...or doesn't She?®

Hair color so natural only her hairdresser knows for sure!™

On a clear crisp day, in brightest sunlight, or in the soft glow of a candle, she always looks radiant, wonderfully natural. Her hair sparkles with life. The color young and fresh, as though she's found the secret of making time stand still. And in a way she has. It's Miss Clairol, the most beautiful, the most effective way to cover gray and to liven or brighten fading hair color.

Keeps hair in wonderful condition— soft, lively—because Miss Clairol carries the color deep into the hair shaft to shine outward, just the way natural hair color does. That's why hairdressers everywhere recommend Miss Clairol and more women use it than all other haircolorings. So quick and easy. Try it yourself. Today. **MISS CLAIROL** *HAIR COLOR BATH is a trademark of Clairol Inc.* © *Clairol Inc. 1962*

Even close up, Miss Clairol looks natural. The hair shiny, bouncy, the gray completely covered with the younger, brighter, lasting color no other kind of haircoloring can promise —and live up to!

TEN
YEARS:
TEN
LANDMARK
COMMERCIALS

7

During the sixties, once television established itself as the dominant advertising medium, the pace of creativity quickened.

The agency that began the creative revolution in print media, Doyle Dane Bernbach, proved equally adept at mastering the new medium of television. They made the transition easily, with skill and ingenuity. If anything, many of their television spots for Volkswagen exceeded print in their impact on consumers. Such commercials as "The Funeral," "The Snow Plow" and "Keeping up with the Kremplers" became instant classics, contributed to the body of Volkswagen advertising lore, and assisted mightily in helping Volkswagen to achieve its sales objectives.

As further evidence of television's increasing clout, consider this: a group of new ad agencies was founded in the middle to late sixties —all of whom eventually grew to become very large and immensely successful—but only one achieved instant recognition and incredibly rapid growth. That one was Wells, Rich, Greene. And its lightning-fast take-off was due to television.

Imagine, WRG hadn't even been in existence in 1966, but before the close of 1967, on the strength of a television campaign created for Benson & Hedges 100's, the agency had already acquired an international reputation. In this new age of television, experience was not a prerequisite for acquiring a reputation, or clients. Experience in what? After all, how many years of experience did *any* agency have in this brand new medium?

To the contrary, youth, energy, freshness and willingness to experiment might well be considered by advertisers to be among an agency's most important assets. These were just the attributes possessed by Wells, Rich, Greene—plus a high-profile account with a big television budget. If cigarette advertising had been ruled off television before the WRG-Benson & Hedges marriage took place, would the agency have been as successful? The evidence indicates that the answer would still be "yes!" Wells, Rich, Greene's consistently brilliant work for Benson & Hedges 100's was not an accident or an aberration. For all of the new clients the agency so quickly attracted, commercials were created that captured the attention of viewers and the notice of the industry. Thanks to TV, before the close of the decade and just a few short years after opening their doors, Wells, Rich, Greene was solidly established as a first flight creative shop.

American Motors *"The Driving School," created for American Motors Corporation, is another of the hilarious television commercials that, in partnership with director Howard Zieff, just seemed to roll out of the Wells, Rich, Greene shop in the late sixties. Like the Benson & Hedges campaign, the work for AMC was based on humor—humor that highlighted product benefits. Every sales point was good for a laugh, but the spot was no joke. It sold hard and effectively.*

INSTRUCTOR: All right. Now let's see if we can find first. No, that's not it.

WOMAN: Ha, ha, ha.
INSTRUCTOR: It's in there somewhere.

VOICE OVER: No matter how rough you treat a Rebel it's awfully hard to hurt it. The survey of professional driving schools shows that they use more of our cars than any other kind.

INSTRUCTOR: How does it feel the first time out in traffic, Mr. Moss?
Mr. Moss? Mr. Moss?

INSTRUCTOR: Look out for that truck!
WOMAN: What truck?

MAN: How am I doing?
INSTRUCTOR: A lot better than yesterday.

INSTRUCTOR: Turn left.
WOMAN: I can't do it while you're watching me.

INSTRUCTOR: Okay. Turn left. (SCREAMS)

INSTRUCTOR: Behind the bus.
WOMAN: What bus?

VOICE OVER: Rebel has held its own against some of the worst drivers in the world. MAN: Sh-sh-should I turn the windshield wiper on?

VOICE OVER: At this point it looks like the Rebels are going to outlast the teachers.

Cracker Jacks *Among the many innovative and ingenious Doyle Dane Bernbach television campaigns of the sixties, none achieved a higher level of humor more consistently than the inspired nonsense created for Cracker Jacks by copywriter Judy Protas, art director Bob Gage and star performer Jack Gilford. As was customary with so many DDB campaigns, this one ushered in a "first:" the first time an adult had been cast (on TV) to act and react in the manner of a child. Of course, that was the very point of the entire series. In this spot, Gilford portrays a schoolteacher who catches one of his young students eating Cracker Jacks in class. That's a no-no, so he commandeers the box, only to be seen a few moments later sneaking a*

few mouthfuls himself. There they were—student and teacher—just a couple of kids who couldn't resist Cracker Jacks.

Using an adult in a children's candy commercial opened up other possibilities for the agency and its client. With Gilford always acting childlike, Cracker Jacks never forfeited its identity, but it did schedule an occasional exposure in adult programs. There just might be some additional business out there. Most important, these spots were so skillfully produced that neither youngsters nor adults were ever patronized, and Cracker Jacks earned the affection of all.

VOICE OVER: When it comes to
Cracker Jacks, some kids never grow up.

Democratic National Committee *In 1964, in a couple of commercials created for the Democratic National Committee during the Lyndon Johnson/Barry Goldwater presidential campaign, Doyle Dane Bernbach once again demonstrated the awesome power of television. One of the two spots showed a little girl plucking the petals from a daisy in a "He loves me, he loves me not" cadence. Then a voice-over begins the countdown— from ten to zero—until the little girl and the screen appear to vaporize in an atomic explosion. The commercial created a storm of controversy until it was yanked off the air. But not before it had further damaged Barry Goldwater's shaky image. It added to a widely held perception of an irresponsi-* *ble trigger-happy threat to world peace. To this day, there are those who believe this spot effectively destroyed any possibility that Goldwater had of reassuring voters who questioned his commitment to peace.*

Although TV had been used previously by political candidates, this was its first dramatic application as an ideological weapon. It featured not the candidate himself, but an idea. For these reasons we include it among the most important spots of the sixties.

CHILD: One. Two. Three.

Four. Five. Seven.

Six. Sev … eight. Nine. Nine …

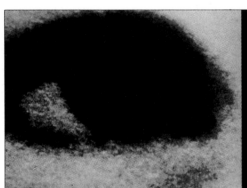

Zero.

LYNDON JOHNSON (OVER):
These are the stakes.

To make a world in which all of God's children can live.

MAN: Ten. Nine. Eight. Seven.

Six. Five. Four.

Three. Two. One.

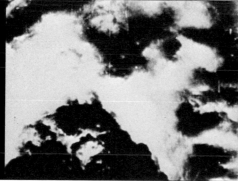

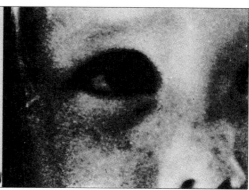

**VOTE FOR PRESIDENT JOHNSON
ON NOVEMBER 3.**

Or to go into the dark.

We must either love each other
or we must die.

VOICE OVER: Vote for President Johnson
on November third. The stakes are too high
for you to stay home.

Xerox *One of the first clients attracted to Papert, Koenig, Lois, appropriately enough, was a new company with a new technology. Its name was Haloid-Xerox. After persuading their new client to dispense with the first half of its name, they urged Xerox to try television. This creative and innovative media recommendation succeeded in waking up most of America to the company's advanced technology. The commercial that accomplished this was more than memorable.*

To demonstrate Xerox's simple operation, George Lois used a little girl to make copies. The spot aired. There were complaints regarding the commercial's integrity. Could a little girl really make copies as quickly and easily as shown? Network officials suggested that George try again, and this time more accurately reflect the degree of difficulty involved. Lois decided to make his point in a manner that could not be refuted and would not be forgotten. In the remake, he chose to use not a little girl, but a chimpanzee. "In fact," he later recalled, "the chimpanzee demonstration was more effective than the one with the little girl. The chimp was a better actor."

There were no more questions.

MAN: Sam, will you please go make
a copy of this?

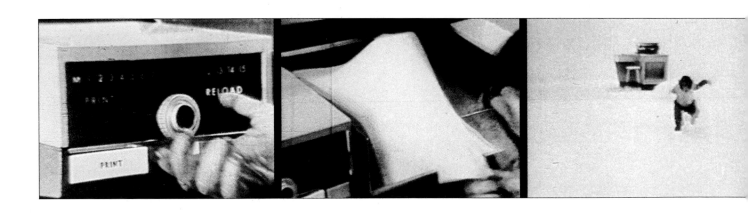

SAME MAN: Thank you Sam.
That was fast. Which one's the original?

CHIMP: Oo oo oo oo oo!

Eastern Airlines *In the early sixties, after acquiring the Eastern advertising account, one of the first assignments faced by the Young & Rubicam agency was the introduction of a new class of aircraft to the airline's fleet. The plane was the Boeing 727, but Eastern held a contest among its employees to choose a name. For the winning entry, management selected "Whisperjet." At the time, most passengers were relatively unsophisticated and inexperienced as regarded flying, and it was not uncommon for airlines to imply that there were differing performance characteristics in the planes they flew. The name "Whisperjet" certainly carried its own message.*

The fact is that Y & R interpreted that name for television by means of a stunning visual statement. In a remarkable commercial produced by Elliot Unger Elliot (EUE/Screen Gems) the whooshing rush of an Eastern jet was merged with the marvelous sounds and sights of the Florida Everglades. The surprised and startled look of wildlife, the sudden flutter of wings and the surge of a muffled but powerful engine all contributed to an image of a modern airline providing beautiful and caring service.

This brilliant beginning by Y & R for their new client set the stage for their creation a couple years later of a truly memorable sixties campaign, "The Wings of Man."

VOICE OVER: To fly.　　　　　　　To rush at the wind and, having caught it,

To come home.　　　　To return to the world again.　　　For the people at Eastern Airlines the miracle,

to climb as high as the wind itself.   To soar.   To hover serenely beyond reality.
To look out to a horizon without bound.

he exultation,   the serenity of flight are a ceaseless wonder.   Come share it with us.

Noxema Shaving Cream *In the mid-sixties, the William Esty agency pulled a neat trick. They transfixed every male in America. And they did it with just one idea that ran for years. The wonderfully sexy Swedish model/ actress Gunilla Knudsen, pouting just enough—with the unmistakable, musical sounds of "The Stripper" in the background—urges her male friend, who is shaving, to "take it off, take it all off." Nothing is removed except shaving cream. But this spot and subsequent variations, aired almost exclusively during sporting events, were so effective for Noxema that they seemed destined to go on forever.*

MUSIC: "Stripper" theme throughout. Very brassy.

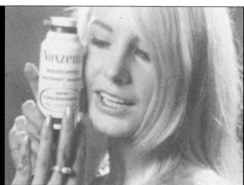

WOMAN: Men, nothing takes it off like Noxema medicated shave.

SAME WOMAN: Take it off.

SINGER: The closer you shave,

the more you need Noxema.

ake it all off.   SAME WOMAN: Nothing takes it off like   .... Noxema medicated shave.

Noxema medicated comfort shave.

Laura Scudder Potato Chips *The east may have belonged to Lay's, but the west was won by Laura Scudder. Commercials created by copywriter Ron Rosenfeld and art director Len Sirowitz of Doyle Dane Bernbach—now principals of their own large ad agency—made a lot of noise on the tube, literally. To demonstrate the product's crispness, each bite was made to sound like an explosive blast. A chubby little boy, before being permitted to snack on the chips, agrees to be as quiet as possible around the house. That's the Laura Scudder "pledge." It's a comic classic that has, happily, remained in memory.*

VOICE OVER: The Laura Scudder Noise Abatement League Pledge.

CHILD: I won't roller-skate in halls.

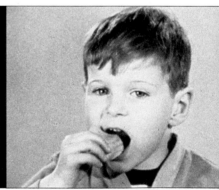

to compensate for the noise

I make when eating.

Laura Scudder's Potato Chips

 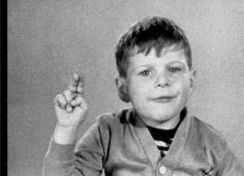 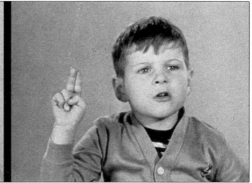

won't slurp my soup. And this I do willingly

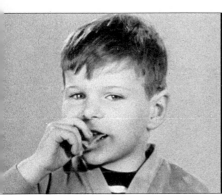 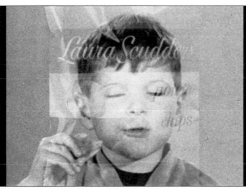 

are the noisiest chips in the world. SOUND EFFECT: Loud crunching noise.

Contac *In 1968, Foote, Cone & Belding did an extraordinary take-off on the lavish Busby Berkeley Hollywood movie dance routines of the thirties and forties. They produced the truly spectacular "Cold Diggers of 1969" commercial, and started a major revival of such dance routines. In sixty seconds the spot managed to capture the look and the feel, and recreated the excitement and precision, of a full-blown, high-kicking Broadway musical revue. It was an extravagant recreation of a bygone era. The likelihood is that the excess of production did more for Busby Berkeley than for Contac.*

(Music to the tune of "Take good care of yourself")

SINGERS: Button up your overcoat when the wind is free,

Take good care of your cold, take care of your cold, you belong to me.

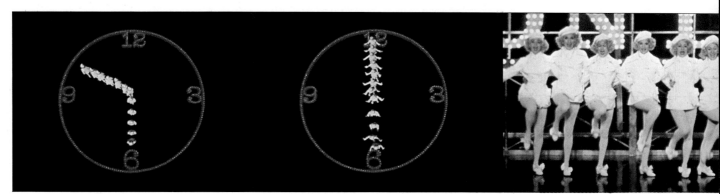

don't go wrong, ooooooooh,

keep those tiny time pills ticking away hey!

So if you catch a mean old cold

Sniffles, sneezes, stuffy nose, don't let them go on a spree, whee!

take Contac, you belong to me.

From the day your nose is blocked oooooooh, 'til it's not, oooooooooh,

lease listen to me.

Quick, get Contac and good bye bye sneeze.

Alka-Seltzer *In this collection of landmark commercials of the sixties we have included two for Alka-Seltzer, one produced in the middle of the decade and the other at the very end. During this span of five or six years, at least a half-dozen other commercials of exceptional note were created for this high-profile advertiser. If Alka-Seltzer, as a client, had any special failing, it was their tendency to believe that better results and greater sales were always waiting for them at the next agency. In the sixties their account was moved around with some frequency, and as a result no memorable campaign was ever created for them—but there were any number of great individual commercials.*

In 1964, seeking a fresh approach, Alka-Seltzer switched its advertising account from the giant McCann-Erickson agency to Jack Tinker & Partners. It all happened just the way Marion Harper had planned when he established Tinker as a wholly owned subsidiary in order to keep restless clients in the family. McCann clients or any other advertisers anxious to sample the new creativity, Harper reasoned, could get everything they wanted from Tinker.

It proved to be a brilliant move, one that paid big dividends immediately. First, Tinker repackaged Alka-Seltzer in hermetically sealed twin-packs. This not only kept the product fresh, but encouraged the use of two tablets at a

No matter what shape your stomach's in … (MUSIC)   No matter what shape your stomach's in

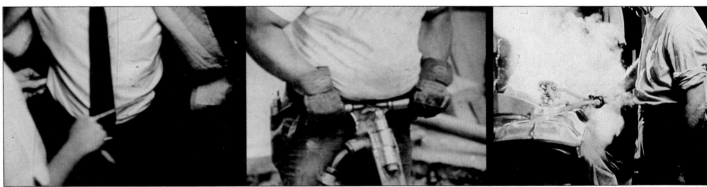

calms the nervous feeling …   relieves heartburn …

time—substantially increasing sales. Then, the new agency created one of the best and most memorable of the great commercials of the sixties.

The viewer saw bellies. Bellies of all shapes and sizes. Jiggling bellies working behind pneumatic drills, sexy bellies left bare by scanty bikinis, business bellies obese and abused—it was one belly after another and an unseen voice suggesting that no matter what shape our bellies were in, Alka-Seltzer could only help. The spot was an instant smash, and Tinker was off and running.

Incidentally, this and the following spot are directed by, you guessed it, Howard Zieff.

..when it gets out of shape

take Alka-Seltzer:

Alka-Seltzer relieves the flutters...

elieves the stuffy feeling...

and relieves the headache. Fact is, today in 1966, nothing works better than good old Alka-Seltzer.

Nothing.

Alka-Seltzer *Although there were many exceptional Alka-Seltzer spots, "Mama Mia" remains our favorite. We're taking a little license including it in this collection, since it was not aired until 1970. However, it is unquestionably a creation and an extension of the sixties.*

It also seems most appropriate to close out our super spots in the same way we began—with a comment about Doyle Dane Bernbach. Toward the close of the sixties the agency had acquired the Alka-Seltzer business from Jack Tinker & Partners, where much great work had been done. After taking over, DDB created a campaign that has subsequently been the subject of much debate.

Following the David Ogilvy party line, it serves as an excellent example of the fact that humorous advertising, no matter how well done, won't sell the product. There's no doubt that this series, although a brilliant and funny advertising exercise, failed to achieve its sales objectives. Those involved in planning the creative strategy hotly maintain that more-complete data would have enabled them to properly target the campaign. Their contention is that modest alterations to script and shooting, with little or no change in humorous content, would have made the campaign the success it deserved to be.

We shall never know.

FIRST MAN: Mama Mia! That's some spec …
DIRECTOR'S VOICE: Cut.
Spicy meatballs, Jack.
FIRST MAN: Sorry.

THIRD MAN: Take twenty-eight.
DIRECTOR'S VOICE: Up Tony. And, action.
FIRST MAN: Mama Mia!
That's a spicy meatball!

DIRECTOR'S VOICE: Cut.
FIRST MAN: Meesy, micey, ballsy, balls.

DIRECTOR'S VOICE: Cut.
THIRD MAN: Take fifty-nine.
DIRECTOR'S VOICE: And, action…. Jack.

DIRECTOR'S VOICE: Cut.
FIRST MAN: What was the matter with that?

DIRECTOR'S VOICE: The accent.

FIRST MAN: A-aa-aaaa!!

VOICE OVER: Sometimes you eat more than you should. And when it's spicy besides, mama mia do you need Alka-Seltzer. Alka-Seltzer can help unstuff you, relieve the acid indigestion, and help make you your old self again.

FIRST MAN: Mama Mia! That's a spicy meatball.

DIRECTOR'S VOICE: Cut. Okay. Let's break for lunch.

THE
GOLDEN
AGE

8 Let's try to put it all in perspective. Creatively, just how golden were the sixties? Believe this if you can: an otherwise sensible, sophisticated and well-informed FCC commissioner, Nicholas Johnson, actually accused the television networks of deliberately conspiring to produce dull programs.

Mr. Johnson intended that his charge be taken seriously. He resisted all attempts to turn his remarks into a joke. Okay, then why in the world would the networks—all three of them, and their producers— do something like that? So that by comparison, Johnson maintained, commercials would appear to viewers to be more entertaining than the programs.

In retrospect, an obviously preposterous belief. But what about the circumstances that triggered it? Were programs really that insipid? Were commercials that inspired? The answer to both questions is, "Perhaps." Programs weren't *that* bad and most commercials weren't *that* good. But many were! More care, more thought, more production values and more ingenuity were lavished on those sixty- and thirty-second commercial gems referred to by the FCC commissioner than on most sixty- and thirty-minute programs.

There were other golden aspects to the sixties, too. Consider this: at the start of the decade, after more than a half century of growth, advertising expenditures in the United States had reached a high watermark of more than $10 billion. It was an impressive sum—an industry seemed to have come of age. But before the sixties had run their course, measured advertising expenditures had doubled to more than $20 billion. The *golden* sixties, indeed!

Imagine, in just ten years advertising attracted as much *new* business as it had realized in the fifty years preceding. For the top ten advertising agencies, which now included upstarts Doyle Dane Bernbach and Ogilvy, Benson & Mather, the golden decade was even more rewarding. The top ten nearly tripled their combined billings, growing from $1.5 billion to $4 billion!

How to account for this extraordinary surge in advertising activity and volume? Just credit creativity? Hardly. The happy coincidence of emerging new technologies joined with the new creativity to propel the ad business to unimagined heights. In just this one short decade of the sixties, all of the following occurred:

1. Television, which had been a black-and-white world, turned colorful in the mid-sixties, in the process completely transforming not just the television industry, but the business of advertising as well.

2. The 35mm single-lens reflex camera matured as a professional tool and it, too, altered an industry: it changed the nature of still photography. Up to that point, advertising photography tended to be passive, with most shoots taking place in a controlled and safe studio environment. Suddenly, location opportunities could be exploited. Photography and photographers could be active and involved. "You could be there when it happened." Experimentation and the ability to shoot and shoot and shoot—35mm photography was quick, mobile and affordable— opened things up for agency creative teams. Photographers could try things with the 35mm SLR they wouldn't even have thought of doing with the bulkier, more cumbersome 4 x 5 cameras that had been in favor before.

Jason Schneider, at the time executive editor of *Modern Photog-*

raphy, was moved to say, "Out of its [the 35mm SLR] potential grew all kinds of things. I think the famous Volkswagen ads—'Think small' and others—came from someone who was suddenly thinking in wide-angle perspective without the use of wide-angle lenses. Arguably, this kind of thing just wouldn't have been dreamed up."

3. Polaroid cameras, like television cameras, suddenly were able to handle color. At the most minimal of costs, art directors were able to play with visual concepts that would have been ruled out before because of the expense involved. Perhaps even more important was the freedom color Polaroids gave to professional photographers. Lighting could be quickly and easily checked through a Polaroid color test. More risks could be taken in setting up shots—risks that would not have been considered before the introduction of Polaroid color. If the photographer had guessed wrong, for whatever reason, the new Polaroid technology would reveal it, and the problem corrected instantly and at virtually no cost.

4. Less expensive color reproduction also had a dramatic effect on the magazine business and magazine advertising. Just as television and photography had benefited from the introduction of new color systems and applications, so did publishing and printing, and therefore advertising. New offset lithography eliminated the costly, heavy metal plates required in traditional letterpress printing. The use of magazine color by advertisers and agencies became more widespread as it became easier, quicker and cheaper to produce. The quality of reproduction was also enhanced in due course, as printers acquired skills and experience with the new presses.

5. There was a host of additional ancillary and technological advances in the graphic arts and the broadcasting sciences that furthered the opportunities for agency creativity and growth. The most visible, of course, were the television innovations: mobile tape units and hand-held cameras, new studio cameras that reduced flare and provided greater detail, complex new editing equipment that permitted instantaneous matting effects to be created, and more.

In the sixties, everything conspired favorably to increase the value of advertising to advertisers, the volume of advertising for agencies, and the vitality of advertising as a commercial art form. The creative revolution was aided significantly by a media revolution that was equally sweeping. Television was now the number one mass medium and the number one advertising medium.

The new technologies and the new creativity converged at a time and in a way that enabled art directors, copywriters, photographers and advertisers to conceive and successfully execute whatever their minds could imagine and their pocketbooks manage.

But all of that still doesn't fully explain the creative revolution. In fact, how does one explain it? For that matter, how does one explain the Renaissance? What combination of circumstances places in one small geographic area, at one pinpoint in time, such gifted artists as Leonardo and Michelangelo, Raphael and Bellini, Titian and Tintoretto? Does the courage and genius of one make possible an environment in which others are more likely to emerge?

This is not to suggest that advertising's creative revolution in any way bears resemblance to or merits any comparison with the Italian Renaissance. Rather, the question is, what can possibly account for so many supremely talented and strongly motivated art directors and copywriters working in the same city at the same time, all contributing so significantly to changing the state of their art?

So complete was the change in the way advertising was created and the way it looked that a whole generation of young advertising people from England and Europe came to the United States to observe and participate in the new creativity. On returning home, in turn, they trained others by teaching Bernbach's principles and philosophy.

Now, more than a quarter of a century later, or since the start of the eighties, London advertising agencies have been proclaiming their creative leadership. The U.K., they say, has taken the play away from the U.S. British creative teams and television commercial directors are more innovative, more daring and more likely to take the risks that leadership demands. If you're looking for breakthroughs, they say, you've got to look first to London.

Are such beliefs fairly held? Are they true? You can get a pretty good argument on both sides of the question, and on both sides of the Atlantic. It depends on whether you're talking to creative directors in the U.S. or the U.K. What doesn't seem to be arguable, however, after close and careful examination of British work, is that all of it appears to be derivative of U.S. advertising in the sixties.

Today, while so many American commercials are devoted to heavy-handed treatments that compare one product with another similar product, or to hackneyed slice-of-life demonstrations, the British have chosen to go in another direction. They've filled their airwaves with humor, sixty-second minidramas and other approaches that had been the exclusive province of Madison Avenue.

In so doing, the Brits have self-indulgently proclaimed their efforts to be "new" or "break-through." In fact, they are not. They are clever 1980s adaptations and applications of Bill Bernbach's well-established principles and techniques. The best of current British work finds its roots in our creative revolution and bears a remarkable resemblance to a whole generation of American antecedents. Only the accent has changed.

For that matter, the most imaginative American work of the eighties—except for pioneering efforts being carried out in computer graphics and simulations—owes a similar obligation to the sixties.

Innovation today, when not merely superficial, tends to relate to technique. It doesn't signal a change of direction for an entire industry, as it did in the sixties. Then, there was a torrent of breakthrough commercials and print campaigns. Today, there's but a trickle. No matter how cleverly we phrase it or how beautifully we photograph it, contemporary advertising for the most part consists of slicker, updated adaptations of the work of the sixties. We're quicker today. We talk shorthand and display split-second images. Some of it looks awfully good. But when television's basic unit was reduced from sixty seconds to thirty seconds (now threatening to become even less), more than time was surrendered to the cost accountants—so was an important element of creative freedom. It's no accident that so many of the better British spots—the very ones they claim set new creative standards—run to sixty seconds in length. This permits character or plot or mood development—or all three—in a way no longer possible in most thirty-second American commercials. Some ideas just can't be executed with maximum effectiveness in so limited a time span.

As we've seen, it requires a rare combination of precocious nonconformists, innovative technology and a spirited economy to produce an environment that rewards risk-taking and risk-takers. But experimentation and exploration of new creative forms is essential if the advertising business is to continue to evolve.

Satellites and cable, electronic publishing and interactive video may already be providing the means by which a new media revolution will be launched. And with the increasing application of the computer to the graphic and communication arts, it is certain that new and creative ways will be found to take advantage of the opportunities that change always permits.

No, it won't be the sixties. But it will be a revolution, and it will be creative—and advertisers and agencies will adapt.

What will the advertising agency of the future be like? And how will the creative team function?

Stay tuned.